Migglism

A Beginner's Guide to Middle Way Philosophy

By Robert M Ellis

ISBN: 978-1-291-87184-5

Published by the author.
Printed and distributed by Lulu: **www.lulu.com**

 Approved by the Middle Way Society:
www.middlewaysociety.org

By the same author:

Practical Philosophy
A Theory of Moral Objectivity
The Trouble with Buddhism
A New Buddhist Ethics
Truth on the Edge
Middle Way Philosophy 1: The Path of Objectivity
Middle Way Philosophy 2: The Integration of Desire
Middle Way Philosophy 3: The Integration of Meaning
Middle Way Philosophy 4: The Integration of Belief (in preparation)

Fiction
Theme and Variations

Poetry
North Cape

All of the above are available from
www.lulu.com/spotlight/robertupeksa

Contents

Acknowledgements

I have received invaluable help in preparing this book from members of the Middle Way Society and others. I am extremely grateful to everyone who read the book, offered comments, or contributed illustrations.

Top of the gratitude list here must be Barry Daniel, who supported the project at every stage. Not only did Barry offer his own comments, but also made contact with further commentators, and came up with ideas for the cartoons. I'm also grateful to Peter Goble and Emilie Åberg, who are also on the Middle Way Society Publications Committee, for initial reading and encouragement.

The cartoons on pages 15, 27, 32 & 53 were drawn by Norma Smith, and on pages 19, 48, and 60 by Peter Goble. Those on pages 71, 77, 108, 127 and 139 were created by me with the help of Toonlet (**http://toonlet.com**). The diagrams were also created by me. The two mules picture on p.40 was originally used by Quaker Peace and Service in pacifist campaigns, and is now, as far as I am aware, a public domain picture. The cover, which also features the two mules, was designed by Barry Daniel and Katja Kaine.

I'm also grateful to all of the following for reading the text and offering comments: Richard Flanagan, Nigel Bulmer, Katja Kaine, Andy West, Colin Cope, Clare Symons, Simon Parker, Ann Foreman, Shane Swift, Eveline and Mike Fedorski, Sarah Jackson, Howard Bramwell, Ed Catmull, Christopher Orme and Viryanaya.

Robert M Ellis

1. Introduction

Peace, we assume, is better than war. A society without slavery is better than one with. A science that shows the earth revolving around the sun is better than one that shows the sun revolving around the earth. But in what sense are they 'better'? Religion has inspired many meaningful and saintly lives, but how can we account for this when it seems so often to be based on *dogma*[1]?

Middle Way Philosophy tries to answer questions like these, and it does so for a practical purpose. In order to make practical progress in our lives, we need some clarity about the theory that supports that progress: for every practical judgement we make depends on assumed beliefs of some kind. Religions and moral systems contain ideas of practical value that need to be separated from accompanying dogmas, without assuming that we can manage with no beliefs at all. Middle Way Philosophy thus brings together practically useful ideas from a range of sources, and tries to judge which are useful and which are dogmatic: a task which is always provisional and subject to further revision.

This little book is a response to requests for a more manageable and practically-focused account of the ideas that I have been developing since 1997, and which have now come to be called Middle Way Philosophy. In 2013, for the first time, I held a retreat for a small number of people in which I tried to explain the core of the philosophy systematically in a series of talks, within the wider balancing context of relaxation,

---

[1] Terms that appear in the glossary at the end (of which *dogma* is the first) are italicised on their first appearance.

meditation, conversation, and artistic activity. I am grateful to the participants of this retreat both for the overwhelmingly positive response they gave me, and for their clear feedback that they wanted more brief, practically-focused accounts of Middle Way Philosophy, as free of technicality as possible. This book is one attempt to respond to this feedback.

The title, '*Migglism*', is an adaptation of a suggestion I owe to Peter Goble, who was looking for a shorter version of the rather lengthy term 'Middle Way Philosophy'. Peter is, indeed, regularly using the verb "to miggle" meaning "to practise Middle Way Philosophy", and others are also beginning to take up the term. The attraction of 'miggle' is its suggestion of babyish mispronunciation of 'middle', and it is thus a way of conveying that Middle Way Philosophy doesn't always have to take itself too seriously. With its practical side comes humour and an acceptance of the childish within us.

Middle Way Philosophy began as an attempt to explain in what sense ethics could be 'right' or 'objective' without appeal to God or any other such absolute ideas beyond our experience. In trying to answer such a question, I made use of insights and practical experience I had gained from *Buddhist* practice, but rejected any appeal to traditional Buddhist authorities and was very selective in the adoption of Buddhist terminology.

These ideas have gone through several phases of evolution. They started off as a Ph.D. thesis, then for several years I was trying to develop them within Buddhism. However, I eventually recognised that they needed to stand independently of the Buddhist tradition. Although I have previously been involved in both

Western and *Secular* forms of Buddhism, I found too many contradictions between the Middle Way and the more traditional elements in Buddhism. I am thus no longer a Buddhist, and Middle Way Philosophy involves no allegiance to the Buddhist tradition, though it acknowledges the Buddhist inspiration of the concept of the *Middle Way*.

Recently, I have been engaged in the substantial project of creating an updated, multi-volume account of the philosophy in depth: the *Middle Way Philosophy* series. This series is now not far off completion. It attempts to combine detail, comprehensiveness, a reasonable degree of accessibility, and at least a fair academic standard of referencing. It is to this series that I will constantly refer readers who want more detailed information, argument, or explanation.

However, the challenge I have set myself in this book is rather different. Setting myself a limit of 30,000 words, I have aimed to identify the key features of Middle Way Philosophy, and why it is relevant and important. Within this length, I cannot aim to convince the unconvinced. If you are unconvinced, please read my more detailed work; or better still come along to one of the further retreats that will now be held by the Middle Way Society, in which Middle Way Philosophy will be given some of the space it really requires to be understood. Instead, I aim merely to engage the curious.

Middle Way Philosophy depends on several interdependent elements, which put together provide a basis for challenging widespread unhelpful assumptions in our society: assumptions about ourselves, about ethics, about knowledge, about science, about meaning, about religion and much else. These interdependent elements are outlined in the first section of this book as "departure points". You could also see these departure points as different inspirations that I have encountered in putting together Middle Way Philosophy, so to reflect this I will approach them with a few personal stories.

Putting these "departure points" together allows us to derive some "core theories" – the second section. The third section, "practical application", shows how this overall approach provides a new rationale for a range of activities that can help us improve our lives. As for a final account of why I believe Middle Way Philosophy to be so important, and how you can engage with it personally, I leave that to the conclusion.

At the end of each chapter I have offered a summary, to promote clarity about the main points, and suggestions for further reading. In most cases some of this further reading is from my own work, to provide a progression of detail for those who wish to look further at any areas of argument in Middle Way Philosophy. However, I have also suggested wider reading from other sources, which may be required in some cases to understand the context of where I am coming from. Rather than using a formal reference system I have tried to give more of an explanation of further reading, with further details of each book available in the bibliography.

As one of the complaints about Middle Way Philosophy is often the use of terms in unfamiliar ways, I have also included a glossary at the end of the book.

I hope this provides an account of miggling that, though not comprehensive, is both accessible and scalable.

Robert M Ellis, December 2013

2. Departure points

Middle Way

In part of my earlier career I was a Religious Studies teacher in a college. I was young, newly-qualified, and influenced by Buddhism. I was working in a small department with one colleague, who was an evangelical Christian. This might potentially have been a recipe for conflict, but actually for the most part we got on well, because we were able to reach sufficient agreement on our educational goals.

However, there was one aspect of my colleague's approach that intrigued and puzzled me. This was the way he coped with the requirement for "objectivity" in Religious Studies as an academic discipline whilst maintaining a strong personal belief in a particular Christian approach. He did this through a rigorous cut-off between the two. He would never talk about his "personal beliefs" in class, and saw his task as teaching the students about "religions" rather than in any sense teaching them religion. At the same time, of course, he favoured factual topics (such as Biblical Studies) that were more familiar to him from his own background.

There seemed to me something very odd and unsatisfactory about this approach. For one thing, it was self-deluded in the sense that his beliefs were always rather obvious from the chosen topics, the way they were framed and communicated, and the assumptions made. For another, it seemed to result in a nervous repression that obviously created tension in him, for he had to hold back his passion for much that inspired him.

Gradually, I began to realise that my colleague, despite his absolute beliefs in God's revelation through the Bible, was also effectively conforming to the expectations of relativism. In the public sphere, where these expectations ruled, no religious view could be accepted as better than another. There were just different facts about religion laid out for examination, and then (so the implicit model went) students would exercise a private personal choice in deciding which belief to select.

This way of operating was largely not the fault of my colleague, but rather the product of a set of attitudes and assumptions in modern society, which he had adapted to as best he could. Faced with clashes between incompatible absolute beliefs, modern "secular" society has often dealt with them by privatising them and making public space theoretically neutral. This disjunction is perhaps most obvious in the US, where religion is privatised by the constitution; but even in the UK, the feeble relics of established Anglican consensus co-exist inconsistently in the public sphere with a large degree of practical secularisation. The neutrality sought in this secularising approach goes too far to another extreme in its avoidance of religious dogma, tending to create depersonalisation, inner conflict, and confusion about how we should make the judgements necessary in our lives.

Based on my previous experience of Buddhism, I felt there had to be a better way. For myself, I felt that I could teach Religious Studies without the disjunctive stress that my colleague was suffering from, because I felt that religions primarily offered resources for a process of spiritual investigation and development. We do not need to relate to religions just as incompatible revelations – and indeed, the more we do so, the harder it becomes to engage in Religious Studies with one's whole experience. Understood differently, the subject could unite the personal with the academic rather than dividing them.

Rather sketchily at that point, I felt that the way forward might have something to do with the Middle Way of the Buddha. By the time I left that teaching job, I had determined to study for a Ph.D. in Philosophy, in which I worked out what kinds of solutions the Middle Way might offer to the disjunction between *absolutism* and *relativism*. My puzzlement about my colleague and the ethos he represented thus created the roots of Middle Way Philosophy.

The Buddha is a historical figure, Siddhartha Gautama, who lived in Northern India about 2500 years ago. It is his life story before he was said to have achieved enlightenment (nirvana) that provides a symbolic account of the Middle Way in experience. Although we have this story from Buddhist scriptures of various kinds, the value of the story only needs to be understood symbolically and does not depend at all either on the historical truth of the stories about the Buddha, or on scholarly arguments about scriptures – so please lay these sorts of concerns aside.

The Buddha-to-be is said to have been brought up as a prince in a palace, where he was indulged in every pleasure and protected from all sources of pain and suffering. However, he was troubled even as a young man with a sense of dissatisfaction with this life, and was also said to have had spontaneous meditative experiences. One day, on a chariot ride out of the palace, he encountered an old person, a sick person and a corpse, which all seem to have represented a sudden recognition of suffering that he must have been denying or repressing. He is also said to have encountered a mendicant holy man, which made him aware of the possibility of an alternative way of life.

Fired by this experience, Siddhartha Gautama is said to have "gone forth", renouncing his luxurious life in the palace, giving up all his belongings and social position, and becoming a wandering mendicant in the jungle. He is said to have been focused on finding a solution to the suffering he had suddenly become aware of, and wandered around seeking the instruction of different teachers to find the right way. After learning from two different teachers but then becoming dissatisfied with their limitations, he joined a group of five ascetics who were practising austerities: bringing suffering on themselves in the expectation that this would lead to rewards in a future life. Siddhartha tried this approach too, nearly killing himself through extreme fasting, but eventually recognised that it did not provide any solutions.

At this point, Siddhartha hit upon the Middle Way. He recognised that neither indulging in pleasure nor practising austerities would help him – but what would help him was to maintain health and meet the basic conditions of life for his mind and body. He would also not find any solutions by going along with the conventions of his closeted royal family on the one hand, nor the absolute ideas about rewards in a future life that motivated the ascetics on the other. By this means, balancing his outlook and avoiding two different types of delusion, the Buddha is said to have attained enlightenment.

It has always been the Buddha's method here that has interested me much more than his supposed results. Given their commitment to this method, I am puzzled by the obsession that many Buddhists, including Western ones, seem to have with the Buddha's enlightenment and the revelatory authority that they believe flows from that enlightenment. I do not know whether or not the Buddha achieved nirvana, still less what that means if he did. Assertions about it lead us into a scholarly quagmire of authority claims, which is not only likely to bog us down, but is also of no practical use to us. Of much greater interest is the method that the Buddha used to make progress, the Middle Way. This method is of universal significance because it can be used flexibly at all sorts of different levels in all sorts of different contexts. It can thus be applied and checked in experience rather than being dependent on authoritative claims made about a person in a remote time and place.

Our understanding of the Middle Way can be reinforced by many other stories about the Buddha's teachings. Perhaps the most important of these is that the Buddha, when asked questions about claims that lie beyond experience, such as whether the universe is infinite or eternal, or whether there is an eternal soul, remained silent. He neither affirmed nor denied such claims, but when pressed said that it was not useful to take a position on them.

The Buddha also used various parables and analogies that encapsulate the Middle Way. A man shot with an arrow does not ask who shot the arrow, what it is really composed of, or where it ultimately came from, before plucking out the arrow – practical requirements come first. A person crossing the River Ganges on a raft does not pick up and carry the raft on reaching the other side, but leaves it on the further bank – so, even if there are some teachings or beliefs that are useful to us, this does not mean they will always be so. A lute-string

needs to be tuned neither too tight nor too slack, but just with the right degree of tension – a direct physical analogy for the Middle Way.

So, the Buddha's Middle Way is the first of the starting points for Middle Way Philosophy. This Middle Way is both an *epistemological* principle (a principal for justifying our beliefs) and a moral principle. According to the Middle Way, we make progress by avoiding different types of claims that lie beyond experience. Claims that lie beyond experience are known as *metaphysical* claims. Crucially, the Middle Way involves not just avoiding positive metaphysical claims (such as "The universe is infinite" or "God exists") but also their negative counterparts (such as "The universe is finite" or "God does not exist"). Since these sets of opposed beliefs involve different types of delusion, to make any kind of progress we need to avoid getting trapped in them.

The Middle Way offers an insight that can help us resolve the problem of absolutism and relativism. We do not just have a choice between the absolute – i.e. accepting a big claim about how things are on authority – and the relative – i.e. denying these big claims and falling back on the conventions of our society. The Middle Way provides a model for how we can *stretch* our relative perspective without trying to jump to an absolute one, provided we constantly resist the temptation to turn the Middle Way itself either into an absolute or a relative value. How this stretching works will gradually unfold. To follow the Middle Way, we need to rest content with the ambiguity that follows when we do not accept either absolute perspective.

Summary
- The Middle Way consists in the avoidance of both positive and negative types of metaphysics
- Avoiding metaphysics helps us to find a way between absolutism and relativism
- The Buddha's life, and some of his recorded teachings, can provide a source of inspiration for the Middle Way, without the need to accept the authority of the Buddhist tradition

Further Reading
There are many introductions to the life of the Buddha available, and most of these make some reference to the Buddha's early life and the Middle Way teachings. However, I have yet to come across a source that focuses only on the Middle Way in the Buddha's life. A

collection of early texts relating to the Buddha's life has been made by Ñanamoli, *The Life of the Buddha*.

Some key references for teachings relating to the Middle Way in the Pali Canon are as follows: *Majjhima Nikaya 63* for the Buddha's 'silence' on metaphysical issues and the parable of the arrow; *Anguttara Nikaya 3.65* for the Kalama Sutta, which applies the Middle Way to judgements about belief; *Majjhima Nikaya 22* for the parable of the raft; *Anguttara Nikaya 6.55* for the lute strings analogy.

For a more detailed account of how the Middle Way can be separated from Buddhism as a whole, see my book *The Trouble with Buddhism.*

Scepticism

My second departure point originates in a semi-legendary figure from ancient Greece. Pyrrho of Elis, the founder of the Pyrrhonian school of *Scepticism*, was said to have travelled to India with Alexander the Great's armies, and thus become a kind of philosophical ambassador, consulting with Indian philosophers. These Indian philosophers may have been his source of inspiration for scepticism. Whether or not this story is historically correct, and whatever his sources of inspiration, Pyrrho did succeed in raising a set of awkward questions which philosophers have since known as Sceptical questions. Western philosophy has been struggling with these questions ever since.

Sceptical questions do nothing less than undermine all our claims to certainty. They force us to recognise that we are flesh-and-blood organisms inhabiting one point in space and time, rather than (as we might sometimes implicitly believe) gods who can look down on the universe and gain an absolute view of it. Everything we think we know about the world has been understood through the medium of our senses and is limited by their range. Our perceptions, even with the aid of scientific instruments, are limited to a tiny portion of the universe. What we perceive then also has to be interpreted by our minds. Time and time again we have made mistakes, both as individuals or as societies, which show our capacity for error. Yet time and again we also assume that we "know" things about the universe on the basis of uncertain perception and thought.

As individuals, we are subject to errors of many kinds, such as hallucinations, misunderstandings, and *cognitive biases* of all kinds. In a psychological experiment, the majority of viewers intent on other aspects of a basketball match did not notice a man in a gorilla suit coming onto the court. Gamblers continue to believe that they will win the next time, whatever the weight of evidence. As whole societies we have made major mistakes in the past – belief that the sun revolved around the

earth, belief that the earth is only a few thousand years old, belief in the innate inferiority of other races. Even scientific paradigms rise and fall. Yet very often we implicitly assume that it is only the fallible people of the past, rather than ourselves in the present, who make such mistakes.

Pyrrho and his successors pointed out that, because of these kinds of constant doubts on all claims, we cannot claim to have certain knowledge. Nor, on the other hand, are our beliefs definitely untrue. It may well be that any given belief is true or untrue – the issue is just how we could possibly know this. Simply because of our flesh-and-blood experience, we cannot know.

Scepticism and its implications have been constantly misunderstood from ancient times onwards, but particularly in the modern period. Philosophers have often seen scepticism as a threat to science, and as something to be refuted or disproved. But it is obviously impossible to disprove an argument that points out that we are flesh and blood from within a flesh and blood perspective. The only useful response is to accept the uncertainty that scepticism makes us aware of. This uncertainty is no threat to science, and effective scientific method makes allowances for it by accepting all conclusions as merely provisional.

Rather than fully accepting scepticism and its implications, however, many modern philosophers continue to battle with it in a way which only betrays an unnecessary anxiety. Perhaps the most influential example of this is Ludwig Wittgenstein, one of the most brilliant philosophers of the twentieth century, but nevertheless haunted by a fear of *solipsism*. Solipsism is the belief that I am (one is) alone in the universe, and that everything and everyone else is an illusion of some kind constructed by my mind. Wittgenstein became convinced that scepticism depends on solipsistic assumptions. In this he shared a basic misapprehension of scepticism with many Western philosophers, who seem unable to distinguish a recognition of uncertainty from the denial of reality. To recognise my uncertainty about the world I do not have to assume that the world is an illusion and thus that only I exist – far from it. On the contrary, to recognise uncertainty is just to recognise that my beliefs both about the world and about myself *may* be wrong. Until I have a better set of beliefs to work with, though, I have to continue to work with an assumed world.

This is exactly what Pyrrho used to do, according to the stories we have about him. He was able to recognise the provisionality of all his beliefs, but this did not prevent him from "acquiescing in appearances". Even a sceptic can acquiesce in the appearance of a glass of wine – not just to the eye, but to the nose and the mouth. In contrast to Wittgenstein's underlying anxiety, Pyrrho was the ultimate cool philosopher, whose goal was a relaxed disengagement from beliefs about ultimate truths or essences and an enjoyment of experience as it presented itself.

Like the Buddha, then, Pyrrho recognised that, contrary to common assumptions, letting go of metaphysical beliefs is of practical help to us and helps us engage with experience. We do need some kind of view of the world (and of ourselves) in order to act in it: for example, I cannot eat my dinner without recognising food and deciding to focus my activity on eating it. However, at the same time, this provisional view of the world needs to be balanced with a recognition that it may possibly be wrong. It is open awareness, not the clarity and fixity of my view of the world, that enables me to notice a stone in the food before it breaks my teeth, or detect the faint creaks that suggest that the roof is about to collapse and that the dinner should be swiftly abandoned.

Pyrrho, too, like the Buddha, combined psychological insights with philosophical ones in his understanding of why it is important to avoid dogma. I can avoid metaphysical beliefs, not by finding some special new philosophical belief, but by holding my beliefs about the world more provisionally. *Provisionality* is a psychological state, which depends on the states in which I hold beliefs, not just on what the beliefs are.

Scepticism and the Middle Way point us towards a provisional philosophy by avoiding metaphysical claims, but the state in which we can really *live provisionally* is one of certain habits in our minds and bodies. One does not become provisional just by claiming to be. Rather, both Pyrrho and the Buddha seem to set us out on a path beset with interrelated philosophical and psychological challenges – challenges that have more often been avoided by academics specialising only in one of these disciplines to the exclusion of the other.

Summary
- Sceptical arguments establish that we can have no certainty about any claim
- Our lack of certainty must not be confused with a denial of knowledge
- Many Western philosophers have mistakenly interpreted scepticism as a threat to science and the justification of our beliefs
- Scepticism obliges us to adopt provisional and non-metaphysical beliefs, i.e. the Middle Way

Further Reading
I give a more detailed account of sceptical arguments, and of the fruitlessness of Western philosophers' responses to them, in *Truth on the Edge* (chapter 1) and *Middle Way Philosophy 1: The Path of Objectivity* (1a&b) – the latter being the more thorough account. I also discuss the classical sceptics, and some of their limitations as well as their insights in *A Theory of Moral Objectivity* 4.b.i.

The original texts for classical scepticism are often fragmentary. There is a useful collection of them in Inwood and Gerson *Hellenistic Philosophy: Introductory Readings*. I also recommend the earlier chapters of Adrian Kuzminski's *Pyrrhonism: How the Ancient Greeks reinvented Buddhism*.

Embodied meaning

At around the same time that I was taking up Religious Studies teaching and being puzzled by my fundamentalist colleague, my wife was studying linguistics at University College London. For her MA dissertation she was studying metaphor. Metaphor is a subject that sets something of a challenge for traditional Western linguistics. Western linguistics is entrenched in a view of the meaning of language as a relationship between an inner *representation* and things out there, and metaphor, not being a 'literal' representation of things out there, does not easily fit this model. However, there must have been a glimmer of openness to other perspectives in this normally very traditional department, because somebody who knew about my wife's interest in metaphor handed her a copy of a book by George Lakoff – *Women, Fire and Dangerous Things* – saying "You might find this interesting".

She did – as, after a while, did I. *Women, Fire and Dangerous Things* is a big, baggy, academic book, and not a particularly easy read for a non-linguist. Nevertheless, it is an important and revolutionary work, published in the late 1980's, with the potential (still unfortunately not fully realised) to turn many of the assumptions of the academic world, and indeed the wider world, upside down. Lakoff takes evidence from linguistics, psychology and cognitive science to show that the idea of meaning as an inner representation of things out there is wrong. It's wrong, not just for the reasons implied by Pyrrho and the Buddha back in ancient times, but also because it contradicts all the scientific evidence about how we actually find things meaningful. *Meaning* is not a picture in our heads, but something we relate to through our whole bodies.

George Lakoff, together with his philosophical associate, Mark Johnson, has developed an alternative account of how meaning works that is more in harmony with the evidence offered by cognitive science. One basic feature of their account is that we can no longer divide semantic meaning (the 'meaning' of a word in the dictionary) from emotive meaning (how a word feels – its associations and connotations). Both kinds of meaning develop inextricably together from early infancy.

Meaning consists in patterns of neural connection integrated with bodily experience as we interact with the world around us. So, for example, as a young child puts a toy in a basket and her mother talks to her about it, she learns the meaning of "in" in relation to her direct experience. Later she sees the bread *in* the oven and is herself *in* a playpen, so she begins to connect all these experiences. This is what Lakoff and Johnson call the *container schema*, a particular pattern by which neural connections associate experience with symbols. The same schema can then be used to grasp other words – *field*, for example, can only be understood with the help of the container schema, because its main common feature is enclosure. Some things are in the field and others not. It's not just words that are made meaningful by such neural connections, but also visible objects and sounds.

Then let's imagine that the little girl is grown up, and is now working as a business executive. In a meeting her colleagues talk to her about *incorporation* and *takeover bids*. She then consults a lawyer, who shrugs his shoulders and says "It's not my field". Here she is still using the container schema, albeit in ever more complex and abstracted ways. The idea of a one thing being *in* another has been *metaphorically extended* into that of incorporation, where a number of people are *contained* by a company, and the idea of a physical field into that of a field of expertise. These complex ideas are meaningful to her in a way that builds on that earlier and more basic experience with the toy and the basket. What's more they continue to be dependent on her interaction with them – the idea of incorporation becomes meaningful to her because that is her work, and she both hears and uses the term.

If we understand meaning in this embodied way, rather than as a picture in our heads or as a social convention, there are immense implications. This perspective can expand and support the understanding offered by the Middle Way and by Scepticism, for it offers us an alternative to the basis of metaphysical thinking. Metaphysics starts with the assumption that meaning is *representational*, i.e that language represents or corresponds to how things are out there. If we really work through the implications of meaning being embodied – both intellectually and practically – metaphysics must perish along with representation.

Why does metaphysics depend on representation? A metaphysical belief is one that must assume meaning that does not come from the kind of embodied experience I have just outlined. Instead, its meaningfulness is supposed to come only from the possibility that it is true or false.

Let's take the example of 'England exists'. 'England' by itself is not a metaphysical claim, just a symbol (in this case a word) that could have a meaning based on embodied experience. One of the ways we might relate to it is using the container *schema*, as 'England' is an area of land enclosed by boundaries, a sort of container that I can relate to my experience of other containers.

If I understand the idea of England, and then put it into a sentence like 'England is south of Scotland' this would also be a claim I could relate to embodied experience. I would directly experience the meaning of this sentence as I cross the border whilst travelling north at Gretna Green.

However, if I put the term 'England' into the claim that 'England exists' this whole sentence only adds to the meaning of 'England' by asserting the general truth-out-there of England. There is no embodied experience that the whole sentence relates to. Instead it just asserts an abstracted idea of a supposed ultimate reality.

The same point could be made about anything else that is claimed to *exist*, or indeed, to *not exist*. To claim that England *didn't* exist would be just as remote from embodied experience as the claim that it did, because we do indeed experience something that we call England, with its churches, village greens, pubs, vandalised tower blocks, and landfill sites. If I commanded you not to think about England because "it didn't really exist", this would make no difference at all to the meaning of England and the impression it makes on you, and you would probably continue to think about it, because its meaning for you has nothing much to do with its "existence". The idea of "existence" is just an abstraction that we stick onto what we experience.

This point will be all the more obvious if we apply it to more traditional and more controversial metaphysical objects, like God. People find assertions about God more clearly dubious because God is perfect, absolute, invisible, and ubiquitous, so to claim 'God exists' is more obviously beyond our experience. Any experience

can be readily interpreted in a way that is compatible with God existing or not existing.

This basic point is the same as the point about anything else existing or not existing. The symbol by itself ('God', 'England', 'the table') may relate to our experience to a greater or lesser extent, but when you turn it into an absolute claim of any kind, it ceases to do so. Its component parts ('England' or 'God') still have an embodied meaning based on direct bodily experience and metaphor, but the further meaning created by the metaphysical claim is no longer based on that embodied meaning.

Instead, the additional meaning in a metaphysical claim comes only from the *beliefs* we need to construct to fulfil our desire to fit in with a group. For example, if we are indoctrinated into religious beliefs as children, we first learn claims about God (such as 'God is the Creator', 'God is perfect' etc.). These do not immediately mean anything to us in the terms we have learnt other meanings (through our bodies). Rather we only come to invest them with meaning by first accepting the *cognitive model* accepted by the religious group. A cognitive model is a coherent set of representations that you could have as beliefs – a potential set of beliefs about the world. If you accept the basic assumptions of that cognitive model then everything else within it falls into place and starts to 'make sense' within its terms. But the way in which you find it meaningful depends only on your acceptance of the beliefs of the group.

This is not a criticism aimed at religion, as religion does not only consist of metaphysical belief, and metaphysical belief is not limited to religion. The same applies to ideological claims made in a political group, or anti-supernatural claims made in an atheist group. Metaphysical claims are asserted as a function of group loyalty rather than because we can affirm what they seem to mean in experience.

Far from being a foundational aspect of the way we have to think about things, as is widely alleged, metaphysics is an addition to meaning as we experience it that we could do without, and be better off without. Not only do we not *have* to think about things in a metaphysical way, but we are deceiving ourselves when we think we are, because fitting in with other people's basic assumptions has such power over us as social creatures.

The discovery of Lakoff and Johnson's account of *embodied meaning* thus added greatly to my understanding of the Buddha's insights in the Middle Way, and his reasons for rejecting metaphysics. The problem with metaphysics is due to the way we try to impose a different understanding of meaning on ourselves when we think in the way it tries to dictate. However, we never really succeed in finding things meaningful in the abstracted way that metaphysics assumes we should. Instead, it becomes an alternative sort of meaning that is imposed on our experience by the groups that have power over us, to try to make us see things in their terms rather than the ones that experience would offer us.

Summary

- The meaning of our language, as well as of art and music, needs to be understood in relation to the body
- The traditional representational understanding of language (that it is given meaning by its relationship to facts out there) is both mistaken and unhelpful, but widely assumed in much of our thinking
- Metaphysics is based on representationalism, and this is part of what makes metaphysics deluded
- The Middle Way thus involves the avoidance of representationalism

Further Reading

I explain the embodied meaning thesis, and many other issues related to meaning, in much more detail in *Middle Way Philosophy 3: The Integration of Meaning*. You can also find both written and audio resources on meaning on the Middle Way Society website.

Amongst Lakoff and Johnson's books, I particularly recommend Mark Johnson's *The Meaning of the Body* as offering an up to date and detailed account of the embodied meaning thesis and the scientific evidence that supports it.

Objectivity step by step

It was reading Thomas Nagel that first got me thinking about objectivity. Nagel is a New York professor of Philosophy, well known for his essay 'What is it like to be a bat?', which got people thinking that there must be something it would be like to be a bat – some inner experience, however strange. He's an analytic philosopher but prepared to question some of the orthodoxies of analytic philosophy – and puts forward engaging though not uniformly convincing ideas. I read his thoughts on objectivity – 'The View from Nowhere' – quite early on in my investigations into Western philosophy.

Looking back at Nagel now, I find many assumptions of a kind that I no longer accept. Nevertheless, when I first encountered him, he pointed me in some fruitful directions that helped me begin to make sense of the Middle Way and its implications. I began to realise that following the Middle Way could be understood as making people more objective.

What does that mean? Well, it all depends on one's understanding of *objectivity*. Objectivity is one of a number of key ideas in philosophy that are used and interpreted in different ways. We have to choose the best way of using it in the light of the purpose for which we wish to use it.

One common sense of 'objectivity' is the one that forms the title of Nagel's book, 'The View from Nowhere'. If you have a view from nowhere, you are not limited by your own perceptions, your own preconceptions or your own position in the world – instead you have an overview like that of God, and see everything perfectly.

Such a view is impossible for us to even imagine clearly, because all our views of anything have always been a view from somewhere. Even if you think about an imaginary land, you will view it from somewhere. Nevertheless we have *an idea* (a completely abstract idea, beyond anything we can actually imagine) of a view from nowhere, and often we call it 'an objective view'.

The other possible sense of 'objectivity', with which I was first struck by Nagel, is what I now call *incremental* objectivity – that is, objectivity gained bit-by-bit, as a matter of degree. This is how Nagel describes it:

Objectivity is a method of understanding. It is beliefs and attitudes that are objective in the primary sense.[2]

A bit later he then goes on:

I shall offer a defense and also a critique of objectivity. Both are necessary in the present intellectual climate, for objectivity is both underrated and overrated, sometimes by the same persons. It is underrated by those who don't regard it as a method of understanding the world as it is in itself. It is overrated by those who believe it can provide a complete view of the world on its own.... These errors are connected: they both stem from an insufficiently robust sense of reality and of its independence from any particular form of human understanding.[3]

This incremental use of the term 'objectivity' is apparently foreign to many scientists and analytic philosophers, but it is used frequently in everyday speech. If someone is indulging in a rather limited view of a matter, we can ask them to "try to take a more objective view of it". That doesn't mean that we expect them to have a view from nowhere, but to be *more* objective. Nagel has hit on the basic usefulness of using the term 'objectivity' in this incremental way. It is *we* who are capable of objectivity, not our theories. Embodied meaning then also makes it clear that the very meaning of the things we can understand more or less objectively is physical, not something you can put in a set of words.

He has also hit on some aspects of the way that objectivity has to be *balanced*, as it does in the Middle Way. If we go to the metaphysical extremes either of those who think objectivity won't help us in

---

[2] Thomas Nagel, *The View from Nowhere* (Oxford University Press, New York 1986) p.4
[3] Ibid. p.5

understanding 'reality', or of those who think it can immediately explain all of it, we will be deluded. We need to maintain a sense of 'reality' as independent of our understanding of it, but nevertheless as there to form a basis of understanding beyond what we currently understand.

This is how I have ended up with a use of language that some people who have studied philosophy say they have found confusing: I use the term 'objectivity' incrementally, but terms like 'truth', 'reality', 'knowledge' and 'certainty' absolutely. I think this split in use of such terms helps us to maintain a balance. Through incremental objectivity, we engage with what seems like 'reality'. However, sceptical argument makes it clear that at the same time we can never achieve 'knowledge' of such 'reality'. Even so, just as Nagel suggests, we need a robust sense of such 'reality' being independent of our understanding and beyond it. This robust sense of 'reality' is required to ensure that we recall that we don't actually have access to it. If that carries a danger of confusion, it is regrettable, but there is a practical purpose behind it which I can't see any better way of fulfilling.

It is this need for a 'robust sense of reality' along with unembarrassed scepticism that has led me to the concept of *truth on the edge*. Truth on the edge is a concept of truth that we need to bear in mind as a meaningful idea at the same time as recognising that it will always remain 'on the edge' of our understanding. It is like something that you think you catch sight of out of the corner of your eye, but when you turn to look directly at it, there is nothing there. Truth is always just beyond the horizon, with perhaps some final oblique rays by which we can still deduce its meaningful presence. We can have a sense of it, but we can never know it directly. That's why I have used the image of the sun just below the horizon as a metaphor for truth on the edge.

Nevertheless, we can have beliefs that are better justified than other beliefs. I am better justified in believing that there is a book on my desk than that there are humanoid creatures called yetis living in the Himalayas, because the evidence of the first is much clearer and more coherent than the second. These beliefs do not amount to knowledge (which depends on the idea of truth), but they provide the basis of confident belief based on the evidence so far. This confidence depends not just on the coherence of these beliefs with evidence and other beliefs, but also on the recognition that these beliefs may be wrong.

But what does it mean to 'recognise' that a belief may be wrong? That's where we need to enter territory that is more psychological.

Summary
- Objectivity needs to be understood incrementally (as a matter of degree) rather than as an absolute 'view from nowhere'.
- Incremental objectivity can be achieved through the Middle Way
- However, we also need to maintain an idea of reality as beyond our experience so as to remain aware that we do not directly grasp it: this is the idea of truth on the edge

Further Reading
There is a further introduction to truth on the edge and its relationship to objectivity and the avoidance of

metaphysics in chapters 1-3 of *Truth on the Edge*. There is also a more detailed account of this area in *Middle Way Philosophy 1: The Path of Objectivity*.

For those interested in analytic philosophy, Nagel's *View from Nowhere* itself provides the discussion of objectivity mentioned above. Beyond this, I have been influenced and stimulated by the writings on objectivity of Hume, Kant, Nietzsche, William James and John Dewey.

Integration

I can't remember the first occasion when I picked up the works of Carl Jung, but I do vividly remember the occasion of a breakthrough in recognising how much he had to offer. For a year between 1990 and 1991 I was working in Northern Greece as an English teacher, and during the Christmas holidays took off to Crete for a couple of weeks of solitary holiday. After a few days driving round the island in a hire car, I found the ideal *pension*, tucked away in the Cretan countryside near the coast, to spend the rest of my holiday. I intended to read, walk and think – always my favourite solitary pursuits. At the English-language bookshop in Athens I had bought a copy of a book by Jung, *On the Nature of the Psyche*, which I soon became immersed in.

I particularly remember one of those brilliant crisp sunny afternoons sitting in the olive groves, and reading Jung's first essay in the collection, 'On Psychic Energy'. Gradually I realised that Jung was offering a completely different view of the mind here to the one that tends to predominate in our thinking. Most of the time we tend to think of our minds in terms of their beliefs or their emotional states, but Jung offered a different perspective – that of energy. Instead of looking at what the mind *is* – always a difficult task given how much it changes – Jung was far more usefully looking at what motivates the changes that take place in our minds.

What Jung means by 'psychic energy' is our total desires and drives in the widest sense. Whenever we want anything, or are motivated (consciously or unconsciously) to think, feel or act in a particular way, energy is the motivator. For example, during the last minute or so, energies have motivated me to think through the words I want to type into this paragraph, and also actually type them, whilst taking sips from a cup of tea. If I were to get distracted, though, other energies might take over, and I might start being motivated more by thoughts about lunch or an email I ought to send. At other times I may become aware of, say, a feeling of impatience or fatigue, which also indicates that energy is going into these channels rather than just into the main activity I am focused on.

Jung's hypothesis in relation to this psychic energy is that it is *conserved*, in a similar way to the theory of the conservation of energy in Newton's physics. In other words, I have a total amount of psychic energy, which may be distributed in one way or another way, and particularly switched between potential and dynamic forms, but it is never gained or lost. This total amount of energy is the sum total of my desires as an organism, and is obviously dependent on my physical energies. My physical energies may dissipate into the world beyond my body, but psychic energies remain within the psyche.

Although the energy I may have at hand to put into a particular activity may increase or decrease, Jung hypothesises that an increase in one place is compensated by a decrease somewhere else. So, for example, an obsessive energy directed towards a particular goal (say, writing a book, or getting a job, or sealing a relationship) builds up potential energy towards alternative goals that is liable to gather somewhere else and then eventually gain expression. If writing the book led to my neglecting the relationship, the need for the relationship might unexpectedly break out later.

Jung's hypothesis is a useful one, though it does not have to work in the same precise way attributed to the conservation of energy in physics to be so. Its usefulness is just to prompt us to expect energy lost in one part of our psyches to still be present somewhere else, and this could generally be the case even if such energy is not always absolutely conserved. Since we have no way of measuring psychic energy so as to be more precise, we have to be content with this degree of inexactness.

Over time, I increasingly came to recognise the ways in which this view of psychic energy fitted with the Buddha's recognition of the Middle Way, and helped to explain why we have a problem with metaphysics. To explain this, we need to discuss the ideas of *repression* and *integration*, which follow from Jung's view of psychic energy.

The idea of repression, widely used in psychoanalysis, is that when we adopt one particular goal with associated beliefs, we can shut out others and cease to recognise them. It is repression, in both Freud and Jung's thinking, that can give rise to neurotic or even psychotic illnesses, as unrecognised energies manifest themselves in ways that continue to be denied by the conscious mind. However, we don't necessarily need to link repression solely with mental illness, nor with the sexual explanations of it that Freud offered.

Repression depends on the idea of the conservation of psychic energy, because the energy that went into the belief that we deny *is still there* even when we deny it. We are not the single selves in control of our minds that we would often like to think we are. Repression can be contrasted with *suppression*, the choice to focus on a particular goal for the moment and put others aside, whilst maintaining awareness of the alternatives.

Obviously, we cannot function without suppression. We have to be able to focus on one goal at a time, and cannot constantly be considering alternatives. That would presumably lead us into a sort of sceptical paralysis. However, there is nothing inevitable about *re*pression. If we can bring awareness to bear on our conflicting desires, then we can both avoid repressing them and bring previously separated energies together: the process of integration.

Metaphysics, then, is another name for beliefs that require the repression of alternatives. If we don't even consider those alternatives, then there is no way we can change our view, so we get a false sense of security from a metaphysical view. But not all views are metaphysical. Some views are held only with an aware suppression of alternatives, which allows us to reconsider those alternatives again when our experience starts to show the inadequacy of the model we have been using. Because of the absolute form taken by metaphysical views, though, they can only be held in a repressive way. For example, you can only believe in your own absolute identity as a self by failing to acknowledge the experiences of other contradictory selves that pop up at different times – or perhaps, in extreme cases, only manifest in neurotic symptoms like *projection*, displacement or obsession.

The model of integration, then, offers an alternative way of thinking about how we gain objectivity. It is more positive than the Middle Way, because it concentrates on ways that we can bring opposing energies together rather than just on extremes that we should avoid. However, it is also the Middle Way inside-out: in avoiding the metaphysical beliefs on either side, we are able to adopt and integrate the more flexible energies that are associated with them.

The way in which integration works is illustrated by the parable of the two mules (pictured). The two mules can represent any set of opposing energies – in other words, any conflict. The two mules at first want incompatible things, and as a result neither gets what they want. However, by reconceiving the way they understand the situation, they manage to each get what they want. They did not need to lose their desires (or energies) to resolve this conflict, only to rechannel them in a way that addressed conditions better.

Every set of beliefs (even beliefs about God or the origin of the universe) contains some reference to embodied experience, and it is only the metaphysical interpretation of those beliefs that we need to reject. Often this metaphysical interpretation is just an unnecessarily rigid understanding of the available alternatives, as we see in the example of the mules. While they were in conflict the mules presumably believed things like "This pile of hay will make me happy", or "I can't help wanting this pile of hay", or "That other mule is just *wrong* to keep stopping me getting my hay".

But there will always be other elements in our understanding of a situation which are not metaphysical, and which we can accept and work with. The mules also had some understanding of how things might be beyond the terms of their initial struggle, or they would never have sat down to reflect and think of a better solution. In doing this they were able to get beyond the metaphysical beliefs that framed their useless conflict.

It is metaphysical belief itself is the rigid element that needs to be rejected, and this should not be confused with the meaningfulness of a belief, nor with our respect for the person who holds it, both of which need to be maintained while we avoid metaphysics. If we can get beyond the rigid interpretations imposed by metaphysics, we may be able to gradually unite energies that were previously opposed. The mules continued to want the hay, and that hay remained meaningful to them in the same way in the solution they eventually reached. They just needed to move beyond the rigidity of their beliefs about things that lay beyond their experience (like ultimate happiness, ultimate *determinism* or ultimate wrongness), not to re-assess the meaning of the more basic elements of their experience.

The following parable may help to bring alive the relationship between the models offered by the Middle Way and by integration. You can think of the Middle Way as being like a ship sailing through a strait between dangerous rocks. The dangerous rocks are metaphysical views, so according to the Middle Way by itself we just need to navigate skilfully between them. However, the limitation of this metaphor is that it only focuses on metaphysical views and isolates them from the energies that go into them and the people they are associated with. These need integrating. So, instead of the ship just sailing through the strait, let us imagine it taking the daring course of landing by each rock to pick up people who are stranded on it and who want to board the ship. It is only after picking up people from the rocks on either side that the ship can go forward through the strait. Once it has picked everyone up, though, all on board are united in urging the captain on through the strait, and no longer argue about the direction of the ship. The people that have been picked up are no mere passengers, but additions to the crew who can lend their energies to the progress of the ship.

Summary

- Our desires can be understood in terms of energies rather than in terms of the beliefs they get attached to.
- It is a useful hypothesis that this psychic energy generally remains conserved, as it does not disappear when you shift attention to another desire
- Energy attached to desires that we deny is repressed (or, if we remain aware of the alternative desires, merely suppressed)
- Metaphysics works by repressing the desires associated with opposing beliefs, and imposing a rigid understanding of the situation on them, appealing to elements beyond experience.
- Desires that are in conflict can be integrated by the adjustment of associated beliefs

Further Reading
There is a general introduction to integration in *Middle Way Philosophy 1: The Path of Objectivity* section 6. The integration of desires is also explored in much more detail in *Middle Way Philosophy 2: The Integration of Desire.* There is also an audio talk on desire and integration on the Middle Way Society website.

Amongst Jung's many works I particularly recommend 'On Psychic Energy' from *The Nature of the Psyche* for an understanding of the basic assumptions involved in treating desire as energy. There is a great deal of other material in the rest of Jung's writings that relates to repression and integration. For a highly readable initial understanding of Jung read his autobiographical *Memories, Dreams, Reflections.*

Brain hemispheres

At Easter 2012 I found myself sleeping in a four-poster bed, with the run of a vast, rambling house in a remote corner of the Isle of Skye, off the west coast of Scotland. I was enjoying the hospitality of Iain McGilchrist, the polymath scholar and psychiatrist, author of *The Master and his Emissary* – drinking his wine, playing his antique piano, and, most of all, appreciating the friendship of one of today's most important synthetic thinkers. McGilchrist straddles the divide between arts and sciences, and synthesises them or brings them together, being a former English literature scholar who then trained as a psychiatrist.

My trip to the Highlands was the rather unexpected outcome of reading McGilchrist's book, and gaining a sudden recognition of a completely different, but complementary, departure point for understanding the Middle Way and integration. *The Master and his Emissary* is a book about the brain hemispheres and their effects, not just on human psychology, but on our whole way of thinking and our cultural development. The 'master' of the title is the right hemisphere, whose role McGilchrist sees as usurped by an over-dominant left hemisphere, the 'emissary'. Grounded on scientific research but also on a deep understanding of cultural history, the book shows many of the same points I had been recognising in Middle Way Philosophy, but from a different perspective.

McGilchrist has revived an approach that many had previously thought debunked. Some previous brain hemisphere theorists have over-simplified or misconceived the differences between the hemispheres, but there is still strong evidence for these differences. The key point about the brain hemispheres is that the left and right hemispheres have adopted specialised roles. This means that although they may have a fair capacity to duplicate each other's functions, they rarely in fact do so. In structure, then, the left and right hemispheres are only slightly dissimilar, but in function most of the time they are very different. The left hemisphere specialises in goal-driven conceptualisation, whilst the right specialises in open awareness. The more each hemisphere habitually adopts these specialised roles, the more efficiently they fulfil them, and the stronger the neural connections that ensure that they will perform them in future.

The left hemisphere has a practical goal-driven focus in both humans and other animals. However, in humans the linguistic abilities of the left hemisphere (centred on Broca's Area) have developed in close proximity to the tool-using centre. This reflects the way in which the human left hemisphere has developed verbal representation *as a tool*. It is only by having a clear understanding of a particular situation that we can make plans to act in it, thinking through the possible rewards and dangers of those plans before we carry them out. Our representation of the world around us also enables us to communicate to others and co-operate with them to reach shared goals, whether these involve killing a mammoth or building a hospital.

So, the left hemisphere gives us our linguistic and rational edge as a species. In some ways it has helped us to adapt effectively to our environment. However, it also carries particular dangers. In order to act effectively, the left hemisphere has to assume that its represented view of the world is correct. That means that it has to lay aside any source of wider perspective, such as recognition that it has held different views at different times, or that it may be wrong in its current view. It is thus very easy for the left hemisphere to get stuck in its view of the world, believing that its representations are literal pictures of how things absolutely are.

It is the right hemisphere that offers possible ways out of this. The right hemisphere is watchful and intuitive. It is more closely linked to our whole bodily experience, where it can relate to incremental changes in time and space. It is the right hemisphere that handles metaphorical relationships between the cognitive models that the left hemisphere can get so stuck in. It is the right hemisphere that can offer a sense of balance and perspective.

However, it is the left brain that is generally dominant over the right. It is the left brain that is the conscious, represented "I", and that maintains desires, plans and identifications. In other words, it is the left hemisphere that is the seat of the *ego* – the ego here meaning the constant *wish* to be a self rather than the self as a fixed thing with defined features. The overbearing egoism of the left hemisphere frequently ignores and represses the more open insights of the right.

McGilchrist's argument is that the left brain has become increasingly dominant, to the detriment of the right. He follows through the history of Western culture and tracks a series of swerves to the left and the right: for example, the Renaissance (right), the Reformation (left), the Enlightenment (left), the Romantic Revolt (right), the Industrial Revolution (left) and modernity (left). The overall pattern in this oscillating history, however, is one of gradually increasing dominance by the left hemisphere. The modern world is increasingly one of legalisation, bureaucratisation, commodification and abstraction – all typical of the left hemisphere and its dry and goal-driven view of things, whilst the intuitive virtues of trust, imagination, and authenticity are increasingly obscured or neglected. Thus we have made astonishing achievements in manipulating our environment, but at the price of our awareness of wider conditions.

McGilchrist's work seems to offer a whole alternative scientific basis on which to understand the Middle Way and integration. It is the left hemisphere that creates metaphysics and gets stuck in narrow identifications that resist integration.

Integration can be understood in physical terms as the development of strong enough neural connections for

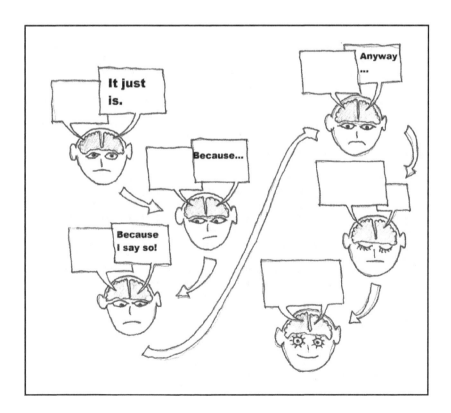

effective communication between the hemispheres. However, what is integrated is not simply the left hemisphere with the right – rather it is the left hemisphere with itself at different times, with the right as intermediary. Since the right hemisphere is outward-facing and voiceless it does not itself need integrating. Rather it is the crucial provider of integration in the whole brain.

The Middle Way does not necessarily need to be supported by this kind of cognitive science, as we can create an understanding of it without any such input, based on internal and external experience rather than evidence about the brain and its functions. However, if one does accept McGilchrist's account, it provides a valuable alternative way in to understanding the Middle Way and how it works. For myself, I am in no position to check the scientific basis of McGilchrist's account in much detail, but McGilchrist references his work carefully, and I have also not yet found any reason to doubt it. As always with theory that offers the hope of progress, I would like to ask those who doubt it what their alternative models are, and whether those models fulfil all the same explanatory needs. The role of left and right hemispheres has been over-simplified at some points in the past, but McGilchrist's account of them is far more sophisticated, and also more far-reaching, than anything that went before.

Summary
- The right and left hemispheres of the brain can be differentiated by their habitual specialisations
- The left hemisphere specialises in conceptual representation, is goal-driven and lacks contextuality, so creates ego-identification and metaphysics

- The right hemisphere provides a more open awareness that is non-conceptual, metaphorical and intuitive, so can integrate the left hemisphere's decontextualised desires and beliefs

Further Reading

Obviously, read *The Master and his Emissary*. I have also written a detailed summary and review of the book, including discussion of its limitations, on the Middle Way Society site.

3. Core Theories

Avoiding metaphysics

Since developing Middle Way Philosophy, I have had to deal with a lot of objections. Some of these come from people who can't understand what's wrong with metaphysics or why we should avoid it. Let me begin with a typical example that might illustrate their objections.

St. Francis of Assisi (1182-1226) is an example of a highly admirable figure, whose life was nevertheless imbued with metaphysics. Francis was renowned for his humility, tranquillity and wisdom. As an alternative to the corrupt monastic orders of his day, he created a new brotherhood and sisterhood – the Franciscans and the Poor Clares. He also had intense religious experiences and courageously tried to bring peace to Egypt during a Crusade. However, throughout that time he remained completely obedient to the Holy Catholic Church and its metaphysical dogmas.

Didn't Francis do pretty well on metaphysics? And how could he possibly have "avoided" metaphysics? Francis can here represent a host of other figures, throughout the ages and including the present, in a similar position. The idea that we should consider the influence of metaphysics on such figures to be a bad thing rather than a good thing requires a complete reassessment of our ideas about religion and morality, to an extent that many people find incomprehensible.

It will become comprehensible only when we look a bit more closely and carefully at what is involved in the idea of a person having a metaphysical belief. The idea of committing one's life to a metaphysical belief is one that has become dominant, not only in religion, but also in some areas of politics, art and beyond: but it is delusory. Somebody who ran their life entirely on the basis of a belief that bore no relationship to experience would not be able to respond to her experience, because they would have no alternative models that were compatible with that experience. She would be in a state of serious psychosis, in which idealised fantasy prevented all responsiveness, and all experience was understood in terms of projection.

Thus, we can be confident that even the most committed saint does not in fact run their lives on the basis of metaphysical beliefs. Instead, they have a number of models of the world around them that they construct either directly from experience, or from the models given to them by others in the course of their socialisation and education. Included in these models are metaphysical ones. Deeply rooted in a metaphysical belief is the idea of the ultimate importance of that belief: but experience does not bear out such a claim of self-importance.

In the case of St. Francis, then, we would expect his main beliefs to be ones about the practical world in which he lived: for example, the lasting and solid nature of objects such as walls and tables; beliefs about social relationships and of what sorts of behaviour were acceptable and unacceptable in medieval Assisi; or beliefs about the political rule of the Dukes of Spoleto and the negative effects of questioning their power. The fact that Saint Francis also believed strongly in the existence of God, that Jesus was the Son of God, and that the Pope was the representative of God on earth, did indeed have important effects on Francis's life, but that does not mean that they were the only or even most practically important beliefs that he held.

Let us take St. Francis's virtues of tranquillity, humility and wisdom, which Francis himself (and presumably

most modern Christians) would attribute to his strong belief in God, Christ and the Church. Yet Francis's actual experiences relating to these things would have come through prayer, in which he may have attained highly integrated states, from a sense of meaningfulness in his whole life, and through encounters with the Church, its clergy and the Pope. When having a religious experience, Francis would have strongly associated this with metaphysical beliefs– but the meaning of this experience was a direct physical one, as we have seen from the embodied meaning theory. The experience itself could not have been based on metaphysical 'truths', because these 'truths' were themselves constructed through metaphor on the basis of prior physical experience. Rather, the metaphysical 'truths' were a rationalisation imbued by the habitual thinking of his society and projected onto the experience. Not even the meaning of such experiences for Francis would be dependent on metaphysical belief, because for him they would mean God – by himself an archetypal symbol of integration, not a metaphysical belief.

So Francis's virtues would have come, not from his metaphysical beliefs, but from his more basic experience of integration encountered in his religious practice. Temporary experiences of integration, especially when experienced deeply on a regular basis, as they are by some meditators, are a wonderful source of tranquillity, of a kind that could keep Francis content with extreme self-imposed poverty. They are also a source of wisdom, because they provide a wider perspective on experience that can open up our judgement and help it take into account a wider range of conditions. This experience of integration would also keep the edges of his cognitive models supple and malleable in a way that would enable him to accept correction by others and recognise his own limitations: in other words give him humility.

Francis was a saint not because of, but despite, his metaphysical beliefs. The very fact that he could emerge in the context of medieval Catholicism tells us something of the strengths of that tradition. The virtues of integration were admired, even though there was a good deal of confusion about their source. It was possible, in fact, to believe that metaphysics was good and that ordinary physical experience was evil – the exact opposite of what I would argue to be the actual case – and to make that belief stick. But at the same time, people would actually make most of their judgements based on ordinary physical experience – including many of their moral and religious judgements.

How has such a belief been made to stick for so long? I can only suggest that this is because it had an adaptive value in maintaining group loyalty. People maintained their loyalty to the Church in medieval times, and this loyalty helped them to live together with limited conflict, and united them against enemies that would otherwise have defeated them. There is nothing better than an apparently unquestionable belief for maintaining loyalty and group identity.

However, this apparently positive effect of metaphysics comes at a price. We can see that price illustrated in Francis's own life. Unable to question the Pope's authority, he remained at the mercy of papal whims. Deeply committed to the ideal of poverty as an end in itself based on the self-sacrifice of Christ, Francis got into conflict with other early members of his order who wanted a slightly less ascetic lifestyle in which a few more of their needs could be met. Francis had his weaknesses, and we can trace each of these directly to an appeal to metaphysical authority.

More widely, the medieval society in which Francis lived suffered from its obsessive relationship to metaphysics. Conflict was created both internally (e.g. putting down of heresies such as the Cathars) and externally (e.g. the Crusades). The scientific advances that had been made in Classical times were largely forgotten, continued and developed only in the (at that time) slightly less rigid Islamic world. Political rule remained autocratic, society stratified, education and learning extremely limited. New ideas were dangerous and ideological change very slow. The medieval world is a warning to us of what a society dominated by metaphysical commitments might be like. Nevertheless, it was neither unchanging, nor incapable of creating striking innovators like St. Francis.

I hope that from this example, the possibility of avoiding metaphysics might become a little clearer. Metaphysics is not a basic set of assumptions that we can't avoid, as some claim. We do often make such basic assumptions, but it's our business to question them and hold them provisionally as far as we can. Nor are metaphysical beliefs responsible for our virtues. We do all have them, to a greater or lesser extent, and will not be able to give them up all at once. However, an incremental approach can work in shifting our energies from metaphysical beliefs to non-metaphysical ones.

St. Francis himself may have got about as far as he could in avoiding metaphysics, given that he lived in such a deeply metaphysical society. So part of the effort in avoiding metaphysics may take place at a social and political level. For example, if we were no longer indoctrinated into metaphysical views from early childhood, this would no doubt help us in avoiding them. However, each of us is placed in a situation now in which we have certain metaphysical influences and certain non-metaphysical influences. We need to work with whatever we have, from wherever we start.

In thinking about this issue, there is one particular opposing pair of metaphysical views that it is important to avoid – these are freewill and determinism. We experience making choices, and we experience various influences on those choices, but to interpret these as pure freewill, in which we could theoretically do whatever we wish, or pure determinism, where we have no choice at all, takes us far beyond that experience. The need to avoid both freewill and determinism needs to form part of our understanding of what it means to avoid metaphysics in general. It's not that we can suddenly 'choose' to avoid metaphysics, but nor is it that we are helplessly subjected to it. Rather, there are a variety of practices (that I will discuss in section 3) that help us to make gradual progress.

Summary
- Metaphysical beliefs are only some of the mixture of beliefs that motivate us
- Practical beliefs predominate even in the lives of those with strong metaphysical beliefs
- Metaphysical beliefs themselves are usually identified with a gross overestimation of their effects
- The meaning of religious experiences needs to be separated from the metaphysical conclusions that are often drawn from them
- We all work with some base metaphysical beliefs, but these neither determine our lives completely, nor can we instantaneously choose to dismiss their influence

Further Reading

This is an area that I am planning to discuss in more detail in *Middle Way Philosophy 4: The Integration of Belief*. However, this final volume in the *Middle Way Philosophy* series is not yet published at the time of writing. In the meantime, you can find audio materials on belief and metaphysics on the Middle Way Society site.

My main source on St Francis is *Francis of Assisi* by Adrian House

Moral objectivity

I have been fascinated by ethical issues for a long time, especially having had the opportunity to teach them to young people. One of the mainstays of theoretical moral discussion is the moral dilemma. These dilemmas construct a scenario which is theoretically possible, though perhaps extremely unlikely, in order to focus on the difficulties of moral choice in certain situations. Here is a stock example.

There is a runaway train hurtling down the track, and it cannot be stopped. You are standing at a junction with the power to divert the train onto another track. On the track the train is currently going down, there are 5 people tied to the track, who will die if the train hits them. You don't have time to untie these people. You could, if you wish, divert the train onto another track, where there is only 1 person tied. This person will also undoubtedly die if you do this, and you do not have enough time to untie them.

At this point, the majority of people say they would divert the train, because it would be better to kill one person than five. A minority say they would not, because they don't want to be responsible for this single person's death, and if they do nothing they feel they would not be responsible for the deaths of the five people.

Then we could change the scenario slightly. Imagine that the single person on the alternative track is a medical researcher specialising in cancer, who has a 20% chance of making a breakthrough that could save the lives of millions of cancer victims. Does this change the decision?

Or imagine, alternatively, that the single person on the alternative line is your spouse, or your mother, or your child. Would that change it?

We could get into all sorts of complexities in assessing the pros and cons of each possible choice. However, there is a single question looming behind any such judgement. What would make your judgement better?

There are many contending criteria that might be used to decide what makes your judgement better: for example, that it obeys the will of God; that it follows a more consistent rationality; or that it maximises pleasure and/or minimises pain.

One of the problems with all such criteria is that they focus only on what you are judging, not on you as the judge. The results when one of them is selected and justified are often completely unrealistic. Most people, in practice, would not be able to perform an action that they knew would kill their own child in order to save others, however rationally acceptable they might think this course of action was in theory. Most discussions of how we ought to judge assume that we are entirely free to judge as we wish, rather than taking into account the constraints on our judgement. They do this because they artificially separate 'reason' from 'emotion' and don't take into account the embodied meaning of the ideas being judged in practice.

The opposite extreme to such idealisation of certain criteria is to claim that there are no criteria that can be justified with any objectivity. Here it would be argued that it doesn't really matter what you choose, or perhaps that it only matters *according* to what you choose, so that you make it matter by choosing it.

Alternatively it could be acknowledged that you are likely to choose according to the values you have been conditioned into believing by your society and upbringing – so, for example, if you have had a Christian upbringing during which your parents indoctrinated you into the belief that every human life is sacred, no person should take life deliberately, and only God justifiably takes life, you would choose to leave the current junction settings so as to let God take the lives of the five people, rather than acting so as to kill one person. Perhaps there would be no choice about this, it could be argued. You would automatically act according to these religious values, but this would not show them to be correct or justified – only that judgements are relative to culture.

Obviously, when applying the Middle Way, we cannot be content with either this absolutist or this relativist approach to the problem. A more objective approach is one that integrates the insights offered by these two perspectives and rejects the dogma. I want to put forward the thesis that objective judgement involves two elements. Both of these are essential, though in practice they will be present to varying degrees:

1. The **consistency** of the beliefs arrived at with other beliefs that we hold, including those about the evidence available to us
2. Our degree of awareness of the **fallibility** of the judgement: i.e. that we could be wrong

Let's look at how the absolutist and relativist approaches fail to match up to these criteria, in order to show conversely why they need to be in this form.

The absolutist has beliefs about how to judge correctly that seem consistent. For example, if you believe that God's will should be followed to judge correctly, then it's quite possible to interpret everything in those terms. God made everything, is responsible for all events, and is testing us in the choices he leads us to have to make, so all we need to do is follow his will. There is just one big glaring assumption here: that we know what God's will is. Now the believer in theory accepts that she is fallible – after all, she is a mere human before the perfection of God – but in practice this does not allow her to take the possibility of being wrong about this one central assumption seriously. Because this central assumption is the whole basis of her world view, and to question it would be to risk undermining everything she has staked on it, she cannot seriously consider it and must merely repress any alternatives.

On the other hand, the relativist is also consistent, starting with different assumptions. The relativist accepts that there is no absolute starting point, but also assumes that there would have to be an absolute starting point to make one judgement better than another. The relativist is reasoning consistently based on these two assumptions.

You might think that the relativist also scores well on recognising fallibility (because she readily recognises the fallibility of absolute beliefs): but actually the relativist is not consistent in their recognition of fallibility. The relativist does not take sufficient account of the fallibility of their second assumption – that an absolute starting point is required to make one judgement better than another.

If 'better' is a judgement we make within experience, absolute justification cannot be a requirement for it. We can require a better judgement to be more objective and more integrated, but to require it to be absolutely objective would take it outside the field of human experience altogether. This would make it both irrelevant and speculative.

So, the Middle Way is really a way of using the fallibility criterion. By avoiding absolutes on either side we keep ourselves open to what experience has to offer. Of course, if we are to make the most of what experience has to offer, we need to treat it consistently as well. But consistency is supported by integration of belief, which we will discuss later in this section. If we combine the models of the Middle Way and integration, the requirements for better judgements within experience will be met.

So, let's come back to you standing at the rail junction. Should you divert the train or not? I'm not going to offer an answer based only on the choices you're considering. However, I am still going to argue that you could make one choice that is better than the other choice. The better choice does not depend only on whether you divert the train or not, and what the consequences are, but also on other features of your judgement.

For a consistent judgement, you need to be using all the evidence available to you (in this case, also subject to a time constraint as the train approaches), and to be interpreting it in a consistent framework. This could be a utilitarian framework, for example, in which you decide to divert the train so as to produce better consequences (fewer people killed). Or it might be a rule-based religious framework in which it would be wrong to perform a positive action that leads to someone's death – that would also be consistent.

However, if we also take into account fallibility, your judgement will be a better one if it is aware of its limitations. The limitations may be ones of information (Do we know for sure that the five people can't get out of the way? Is my view of them a bit unclear?). They may be limitations of theory. The utilitarian framework that demands that you save more lives is not the only possible one. If you have time to consider alternatives (which you probably wouldn't in this case), you could try to take into account the limitations of that framework. For one thing, it puts a lot of emphasis on your capacity to make the right decision based on evidence. If you know your capacity to be poor for whatever reason, you might be better just following rules of thumb. There may also be limitations on the state of mind in which you make the judgement. Are you in an obsessive or blinkered state of mind where you might ignore something important? Is your judgement otherwise impaired?

In short, making a better judgement in this case, as in any other judgement, depends on your awareness, not just of the situation and the principles you want to apply to it, but of the limitations of those principles. If you want to avoid turning those principles into dogmas, you need to be able to bring experience to bear on weighing them up.

What would I do? With very little time in which to decide, and having reasonable confidence in my judgement and that I have a correct view of the situation, I would probably divert the train. However, that doesn't mean that I think this would necessarily be the better judgement for others to make. It does mean that in this situation, I think that a model that tried to take into account the consequences – especially when they are severe consequences that involve losing life – would be the most objective one to apply. That doesn't make me a utilitarian, because I wouldn't advocate that model in every situation. Also, because I can make that judgement by imagining the situation, does not mean that in the actual stress of such a situation I would necessarily be capable of making such a judgement in time. Whether I could think clearly and respond calmly would depend very much on my mental and physical state in the situation.

This example is obviously one of moral judgement, yet the approach I am discussing applies to all kinds of judgement. To relate it to other kinds of judgements will require me to first discuss different aspects of objectivity, as I will in the next chapter.

Summary

- A widespread limitation of theories about how we should make moral judgement is that they focus only on the object of judgement rather than including the judge
- Understanding the right choice in terms of overall principles regardless of the specifics of the situation involves the absolutist's mistake. Believing that there is no right choice is the relativist's.
- A justifiable moral judgement depends on both coherence of beliefs and awareness of the fallibility of the judgement
- For moral objectivity we need to be able to judge one choice in a specific situation as better than another, fully recognising the uncertainty of that judgement (and thus following the Middle Way, avoiding the certainties of metaphysics)

Further Reading

For a detailed account of the theory of moral objectivity in Middle Way Philosophy, see *Middle Way Philosophy 1: The Path of Objectivity*, section 7. There are also introductions in chapter 6 of *Truth on the Edge* and chapter 1 of *A New Buddhist Ethics* (despite the title, this is about Middle Way Ethics rather than traditional Buddhism).

The moral dilemma of the railway junction is a stock example from introductions to ethics. There are lots of these available. Amongst these I would particularly recommend the work of Peter Singer, and Mary Midgley's *Can't we make moral judgements?*

Scientific objectivity

In August 2000, I spent a week on a US college campus at no expense, surrounded by friendly people, who insisted on ferrying me half a mile by car across the campus when I preferred to walk, and subjected me to a barrage of abstract metaphysics. I was making my first ever trip to the US, funded by my first ever prize. I had won the Charles Wei-Hsun Fu Essay Prize, and been funded to attend the '4th Symposium on Field Being and the Non-Substantialistic Turn' at Fairfield University, Connecticut, and deliver my paper there.

The symposium was founded and run by Professor Lik Kuen Tong, a charming and spry elderly Chinese philosopher, who had such a flexible monistic (i.e. all is one) philosophy that he had managed to convince the powerful Jesuits running his private university to fund his symposium, and a broad range of 'non-substantialistic' metaphysicians to attend it. I have just found out that Tong died in 2012, which is doubtless why the annual symposia have ceased. However, I can't say that I found most of the symposium particularly rewarding. Most of the papers developed abstract metaphysics for their own sake, and had little clarity and no apparent practical application.

The paper I was there to deliver was on "Lakatos and Non-dualistic ethics", and was about the ways in which the work of Imre Lakatos, a philosopher of science, could be used to support an understanding of ethics. This was one of the early indications of my growing conviction that scientific and moral objectivity went hand in hand. However, I was unable to deliver enough of my paper for the argument to hang together because of the time guillotine that was imposed, and what I managed to give was met with some bemusement. One of the attendees who had a background in physics ambled over to me at the pizza party that evening and started a conversation about science, on the evident assumption that I was a fellow-scientist, then rapidly ambled off again when he realised that he was mistaken and I was a mere ethicist.

Despite the limitations of my education, which had been based on the arts and humanities, I nevertheless got deeply engaged in the philosophy of science at that time. It seemed to me that the kind of route to objectivity suggested by philosophers like Popper, Lakatos and Kuhn was far more fruitful for ethics than anything going on in moral philosophy. Moral philosophy, it seemed, had pretty much given up on the idea of objectivity, and consisted just of analysing what people generally believed, or working out the implications of a view that had to be adopted on trust. However, Popper had put forward the important idea that we make progress towards objectivity by ruling out what we don't know, whilst Lakatos and Kuhn had developed this by testing it out against examples of how scientists make advances in practice.

It was Lakatos who made it clear that science generally proceeds by way of 'research programmes'. A research programme has an overarching theory (for example, Quantum Physics or Evolutionary Biology) with lots of lesser applications. Scientists will generally focus on a specific application of the overall theory, with auxiliary assumptions, and make predictions about the evidence that should be observed given that application. For example, they might construct computer models of gradual changes in the development of the eye between species, to check its compatibility with evolutionary theory. If they don't find the evidence they expect, they will alter the specific application of the theory, not the whole research programme.

Nevertheless, looking at the evidence alone is never entirely conclusive, and both Lakatos and Kuhn admitted this. One's interpretation of evidence is still dependent on prior assumptions, and scientists are always subject to *confirmation bias* because they will seek out confirmations of their theory and ignore other information. For example, in showing how the development of species through time is continuous and thus compatible with evolutionary explanations, there will always be larger or smaller gaps in the record or 'missing links'. You could choose to take these seriously as making the whole theory problematic, or you could judge it 'reasonable' to assume that there was a link but we just don't have access to evidence of it. A determined opponent of a scientific theory, focusing only on evidence, can always apply selective scepticism to undermine it, as there are always limitations in the relationship between the theory and the evidence.

There will always be gaps in evidence that we have to make 'reasonable' judgements about. But what makes judgements reasonable? Unlike Lakatos, I think we need to take psychology into account in giving an account of reasonable judgement. I have already explained the kind of criteria of objective justification that I would apply in the previous chapter: coherence and recognition of fallibility. A theory can be coherent in relation to other theories, and fit the evidence, but the fallibility of the theory can only be judged in terms of the integration of the person making the judgement. Although Popper and Lakatos tried to explain fallibility entirely in terms of evidence, as falsifiability of a theory, they did not succeed. This is really to be expected given their representationalist assumptions, which involved the impossible expectation of a perfect fit between a theoretical model expressed in language and the reality of the universe.

Our judgements about the fallibility of a scientific theory involve the same process as our judgements about a moral theory. In each case we need to be aware of alternative possibilities, so that we can compare those alternatives to the evidence of experience when a problem arises with the current theory. This awareness is *provisionality*. To be held provisionally, a theory has to allow for such alternatives, rather than allowing us to experience them as a threat that must be repressed. A theory that can only be held through such repression is a metaphysical theory that cannot be provisional. Even a scientific theory that we take for granted, such as the law of gravity, needs to be held provisionally. We can assume neither complete proof nor complete disproof from limited evidence.

Most commonly, it is specific sub-theories rather than overarching 'research programmes', 'paradigms', or 'moral traditions' that are subject to change in this way. But the overarching theories also need to be provisional. Lakatos wrote about research programmes becoming 'unfruitful' because they no longer yielded useful predictions that could be tested, when compared to alternative overarching theories. There is no sudden moment when an old paradigm disappears. For example, the geocentric view of the universe did not crumble into dust at one moment, or even in one afternoon. Rather such theories gradually lose momentum as people change their practical allegiance and cease to work in terms of that theory. People tried out the Copernican system, in which the earth revolves around the sun, and found it much more fruitful. It is the

comparison with another overarching theory, judged over a period of time, that is required to let go of it.

Scientific objectivity, then, needs to be understood in terms of the judgements of scientists, as developed through the culture of scientific method, rather than in terms of the representational correctness of the theory. That objectivity puts science in line with ethics and also with aesthetic judgements. In practice, there is no distinction between 'facts' and 'values'. The kind of judgement being made, and the considerations that make it objective, are not different. They are just being applied in different spheres.

There are some indications that science is itself recognising the limitations of a view of itself based only on representation, and trying to compensate for it. Complexity theory, for example, considers the ways in which networks (e.g. of neurons, or creatures in an ecosystem) have so many complex inter-relationships that they are radically unpredictable. If we are to get to grips with such complexity and unpredictability, we have to change our approach to judgement: it becomes not just a question of applying a 'correct' model, but more of finding a balanced point between the model one is using and the chances of it being wrong. Our understanding of scientific objectivity is thus increasingly developing some of the features often allocated to moral judgement.

It could even be argued that we are now entering a *third phase* of human thought. In the first, medieval, phase, scientific objectivity was limited by its subjection to moral metaphysics. In the second, modern, phase, conclusions were drawn by relating observation to theory, and ethics was made irrelevant. In the third phase of human thought which I hope may be dawning, science and ethics will be seen as unified, with objective judgement in each involving a process of balancing out models with the chances of those models being wrong.

Summary
- Philosophers of science have established that there will always be gaps of assumption in the way in which scientists use evidence to support theory
- We have to rely on the judgement of scientists (both individually and collectively) to support the objectivity of theories
- This means that the objectivity of science, like that of ethics, is dependent on provisionality of judgement and is incremental
- There is thus no distinction between moral and scientific objectivity: they can be judged in the same way, merely applied in different spheres

Further Reading
For a more detailed discussion of different types of objectivity and their relationship, see *Middle Way Philosophy 1: The Path of Objectivity* section 4. There is also a discussion of the process of scientific discovery in *A Theory of Moral Objectivity* 2.b, and of scientific progress in *Truth on the Edge* chapter 7.

For an understanding of how the philosophy of science can support this perspective, I recommend Thomas Kuhn's *The Structure of Scientific Revolutions* and Imre Lakatos's 'Falsification and the Methodology of Scientific Research Programmes'.

How integration works

It is the process of integration that allows us to recognise fallibility, for it is only as we recognise the limitations of one cognitive model that we can let our guard down sufficiently to unite it with another. Much of my own direct experience of how this happens comes from meditation.

I first learnt to meditate as a fresh undergraduate student at Cambridge, keen to try out everything. During my first few days as a fresher I met a flamboyant theologian with a Sanskrit name, an ordained Buddhist who invited me to a Buddhist meditation class. This turned out to be the beginning of a personal practice that persists to this day: a practice that is rarely profound but nearly always helps to balance my mental states and limit my tendency towards obsessive certainty.

The first step in meditation is always to relax one's body sufficiently, so that it becomes heavy, and physical restlessness falls away, at least temporarily. One also seeks a posture that is upright and open-chested without being rigid, which together with physical relaxation can enable feelings of energy to run up the body. At the same time one needs to focus on the object of the meditation: which in the case of my own habitual practice is usually the breath. The focus on the object, relaxation and physical energy all need to work together so that one inches into a relaxed and concentrated state and leaves behind anxious, angry or desirous thoughts. Not that one leaves behind thought (this is a common misunderstanding of meditation), but that one's thoughts become more aware, spacious and under control.

The point of meditation, just like the point of science, is not to get to a 'truth', but to make incremental progress in avoiding delusion. In meditation that delusional state is represented by distraction, and progress is made by working with one's distractions rather than by reaching any kind of positively ideal state. One can work with distractions in two kinds of ways: relaxation and stimulation. Each of these ways will need to be carefully targeted.

For example, if I am buzzing with anxious thoughts about someone I need to communicate with in a challenging way, I will need to relax those thoughts by bringing my awareness much more into my body. Since all meaning is embodied, I can put the meaning of those anxious thoughts into a bigger context, without denying or blocking them, by relaxing their meaning into a bigger bodily meaning. Once that bodily awareness is more fully achieved I can start to return to the object of meditation.

On the other hand, if I am too placid and experience little energy in meditation, there is a danger of sleepiness. In this kind of circumstance it is a sharper and more focused meaning that is needed in my meditation. Focusing more strongly on the object of meditation will help here. If I am focusing on the breath, I look for sharp and vivid experiences of energy in my sensations of the breath as they enter the nostrils.

Meditation is a constant process of adjustment and re-adjustment. One begins to get into the meditation, then gets distracted, then makes adjustments. However, as soon as I start to feel I am succeeding in some way, most likely another distraction will gradually start to creep in. In a similar way just as when a scientist feels that he has discovered the final definitive laws of nature, some challenge will creep in somewhere else, and just as when we feel we have the correct moral answers, our certainty will begin to be undermined by alternative moral perspectives from elsewhere.

I can make gradual progress in meditation, not only by entering an increasingly coherent meditative state, but also by maintaining a sense of fallibility. I always need to be subtly on my guard against the possibility of falling back into distraction. As I make such progress, I am entering a state of temporary integration. This means that, to some degree and for the moment, my energies are increasingly working together, rather than against each other like the two mules. The model of the world that I am working with also becomes one that encompasses a wider picture, within which those energies can be reconciled, just as the two mules managed to fulfil both their desires by reconsidering the situation. When they start working together, the two mules maintain an increasingly coherent representation of their situation. However, they would never have been able to reconsider their situation at all if they had not had some sense of the fallibility of their previous view.

When a distraction is overcome in meditation, it is like one of those mules. Imagine one mule wanting to do the meditation and focus on the breath, whilst the other wants to think about breakfast instead. They have a tug-of-war, and sometimes one starts to 'win', sometimes another, but they remain frustrated because neither does the meditation improve, nor is the desire for breakfast fulfilled. Finally, the meditator gets in touch with a sense of fallibility. The desire to meditate cannot be fulfilled without taking into account the desire for breakfast, but a life in which one only thought about breakfast and made no progress in meditation would also be less satisfying. The answer is thus to focus fully on meditation first, then finish meditation and have breakfast. With that awareness, the two energies can

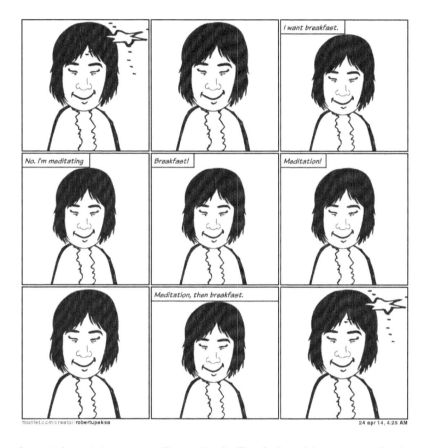

be at least temporarily united. Each is able to eat their bale of hay at a time.

Then think about the similar position of a scientist, or perhaps a group of scientists working together on a research project. Here the two desires involve on the one hand loyalty to a theory, and the other hand the potential distraction of evidence that could be interpreted in a different way contrary to that theory (perhaps with an alternative theory to explain it). Each could ignore the other, and the tug-of-war could continue. The scientists could continue with their project, but niggling doubts will continue to undermine it. Or the scientists could allow themselves to be diverted into an alternative channel by the exploration of apparent counter-evidence and the need to explain that counter-evidence. In order to be able to integrate those energies, they need to be seen as part of a larger picture. The exploration of counter-evidence needs to be not just a gesture towards open-mindedness, but it needs to be appreciated that this exploration actually contributes substantially towards the research project. The research project, after all, will not be fulfilled by finding a truth of nature, but rather by effectively investigating counter-arguments, and taking them into account in an increasingly objective theory.

Or let us compare this with another dilemma: that of an artist. This artist has been working in one kind of medium for some time: let's say a particular style of abstract painting. It is quite satisfying, is explored with a growing sense of meaning, and is helping her sell a few pictures. However, more recently an alternative desire has begun to niggle at her: a desire to explore a rather different medium. There is the occasional sense that she is stuck in a groove with abstracts. Perhaps she could try sculpture, or collage, or representational painting. This dissatisfaction with her current medium is beginning to disrupt her focus on her work. Again, the two mules could have a tug-of-war. The satisfaction with current work could continue to be undermined, and yet no new kind of work could be started. She needs to find a new vision of her work that will encompass both the old form and some new kind of form.

Integration, then, is a basic feature of human experience, and a basic way in which people increase the objectivity of their judgements. If we only bring metaphysical beliefs to these judgements, the two mules will carry on stubbornly tugging at each other, and no progress will be made. If on the other hand we are able to bring a sense of fallibility as well as a coherence of view to our judgements, it is possible both for our beliefs to gain an increasing long-term objectivity and our desires to become increasingly focused in effective ways.

Integration, then, is not just a state of psychological health. Nor is it limited to aesthetic, moral, or scientific judgements. Rather it provides a model for the process by which objectivity can be achieved at every level of human experience. It can be applied from the most reflective individual experience, as in meditation, and also to political, social and scientific debates that involve large number of people.

The basic reason why integration works, and why it provides a model for objectivity, is that it is consistent with universal experience. Meditation is a good place to start only because it obliges us to focus on that experience free of distraction in a way that few other activities do. But there is nothing magic about meditation and no 'truths' to be discovered in meditation. The process of integration depends at every point on an acceptance of uncertainty and ignorance.

Summary
- Integration occurs through the relaxation of opposing desires and consideration of opposing beliefs

- The process of integration does not involve discoveries of 'truth', but rather the gradual ruling out of alternatives so that energy can increasingly be focused in one area
- A balance (the Middle Way) is always required between maintaining current desires and beliefs and consideration of challenges – coherence and fallibility

Further Reading

The process of integration is discussed in more detail in *Middle Way Philosophy 2: The Integration of Desire* section 2. There is also more detail on the practice of integration in section 4.

For more recommendations about meditation, see the chapter on meditation in section 3 below.

Levels of integration

There is a striking scene in the film 'Gandhi' in which wave upon wave of peaceful Indian demonstrators advance upon armed policemen. Each wave is beaten back, and not one person fights back, but the waves of protesters nevertheless continue with not the slightest loss of resolution. The demonstrators had been carefully trained by Gandhi in the techniques of passive resistance.

What is particularly important about such scenes is the way in which they communicate Gandhi's insights into conflict. Although I do not agree with Gandhi's metaphysical beliefs, he also had some valuable practical ones. Prime amongst these is the perception that a person who is your opponent, or even your oppressor, is not your enemy. Thus your campaign needs to be directed not against him or her as a person, but against the beliefs that pitch their desires against yours. Harming another is most likely to entrench the conflict, so it is much more valuable to persuade than to harm. One effective way of persuading may sometimes be to voluntarily take the harm upon yourself.

This is a good example of integration at the socio-political level, where it can apply just as much as at individual level. At both levels, similar conditions apply. There are competing desires that gain dominance at different times, both in the individual and in wider society. Those desires are attached to beliefs representing the world in which the individual or society is moving. Those desires can continue to vainly compete, each with incompatible beliefs, or they can move into more appropriate beliefs and integrate. Just as the two mules can fight or integrate, so can two nations – and indeed, the mule pictures were originally created by pacifists and labelled 'a fable for the nations'.

The desires held by groups or societies are always simultaneously the desires held by individuals. A clash between groups, even on the scale of world war, is nothing more nor less than a clash of desires. This offers a crucial insight: whenever you get into conflict with someone else, you are not fighting them as an individual, but rather fighting their desires. In a conflict of desires, indeed, there can be no enemies.

There are, of course, also differences between the integration of the individual and of society. Generally, however, it is the similarities that are under-appreciated, because of our resistance to recognising that we may not be single selves, leading to a preference for thinking of 'me' as one self in opposition to other selves. The constant pressure of the ego is to maintain the belief in a single self, which assumes that we are already integrated, and that it is only society beyond us that needs integrating. This can only be described as a massive delusion. Of course society does need integrating, but so do we as individuals.

Those who have compared the individual to a city, with different competing citizens, have often been considered rather fanciful. However, the likely accuracy of a view of ourselves as plural is confirmed not only by the observation of psychological disorders (such as multiple personality disorder) in which selves are identifiably separate, but by psychoanalysis, by conflicts between the two brain hemispheres, and by the crucial role of metaphorical constructions in meaning under the embodied meaning thesis (showing that there is no single 'correct' metaphor under which we work). If the individual is like a society, then, the society is also like an individual, because it can become more or less unified. The macrocosm (society) can be constantly compared to the microcosm (individual).

The macrocosm and microcosm are similar not because of some essential feature of each, but because of a similarity in their structure. Both are best understood as networks rather than separate objects. A society is a network of individual people, but an individual person is a network of neural connections interacting through a body. Just as the larger network of society is subject to variations in openness or exclusivity, unity or division, so is the smaller one within the body.

The main difference between the processes of integration of the individual and society is just that the process in society has a further level of complexity. Desires in society may be pursued by individuals, or by groups of varying sizes, all competing with each other. Groups can exist at different levels, from the family unit to the nation state, and larger groups may consist of hierarchies of shifting sub-groups. A degree of integration in a larger group is dependent on that of sub-groups, which is in turn dependent on the integration of individuals.

To make this situation even more complex, we are all members of many different groups. For example, a male middle-aged Sikh physics teacher living in Birmingham who is married with a family and likes model railways, is a member the group of males, the group of middle aged people, the local, national and international Sikh community, the group of teachers, the group of physics teachers, the group of Birmingham residents and also residents of his specific neighbourhood, the group of British citizens, the group of his immediate and wider family, the group of husbands, the group of fathers, and the group of model railway enthusiasts. These are just formal groups: he may also have informal groups of friends, or be part of further online social groups. All that is required to make one a member of such a group is identification with it.

Any of these complex groups that we are part of may be more or less integrated, insofar as the desires of the members are compatible or incompatible in relation to the group. They will only be compatible to the extent that the relevant beliefs are shared. So, for example, if teachers are divided over whether to go on strike about changes to their pension scheme, this means that the group of teachers has different beliefs about justified action in the situation, and because of these different beliefs, like the two mules, they are tugging the group of teachers in incompatible directions.

To think about the integration of groups within a wider society or nation thus potentially brings in enormous complexity. Not only will there be competing desires, with some dominant over others, in that society as a whole, but some of these desires will be dominant in big groups and smaller groups within that society. These groups in turn will be composed of individuals who each have competing desires within them, some of which will be dominant at a given time and others repressed. The desires that end up dominating in the society as a whole will be those of certain individuals, who manage to get their desires to dominate smaller groups, which dominate bigger groups, and so on. The diagram below gives a simplified schematic view of this situation. Here different desires are represented by different textures. The plain grey desire has ended up dominating the whole society in this case, even though only two indivi-

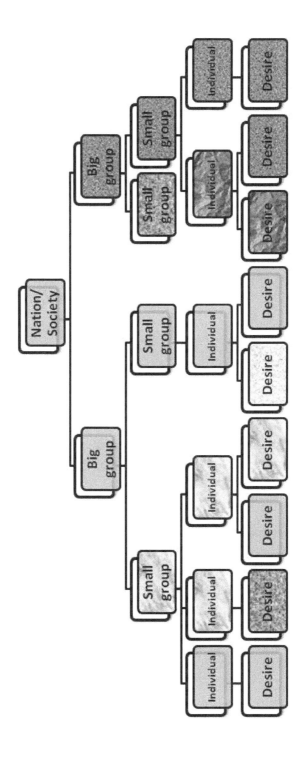

-duals on the diagram hold that desire (and one of them is also repressing other desires).

Nevertheless, we may need to integrate conflicts at a social and political level, even if we are only able to do so crudely, in order to address them effectively at an individual level. Most of the desires held by individuals will be ones understood and articulated in relation to groups. For example, the individual may have a desire for better rights of fathers for custody of children in divorce cases, or a desire for electoral reform, as well as a desire for pudding or a desire for sex. Even something as basic as a desire for sex will nevertheless by mediated by social models and expectations.

Given the amount of complex interplay between our desires at individual level and at social level, we have no option but to engage in integration at both levels simultaneously. There is no choice between individual and social integration, for neither is likely to get very far without the other. We need our outer Gandhis to bring integration to a political conflict, but we also need an inner Gandhi to confront the shadows within ourselves with insight, compassion and resolution.

Summary
- Conflicts at both individual and social level are all still conflicts of desires, and should be seen as such, rather than as conflicts between individuals or groups
- Integration (and thus following the Middle Way) at individual and social levels is thus basically the same process

- Integration at group level is potentially much more complex because there are many different layers of conflict to consider

Further Reading
There is further discussion of integration at group level in *Middle Way Philosophy 1: The Path of Objectivity* 6.f, and of socio-political integration in *Truth on the Edge* chapter 9 and *Middle Way Philosophy 2: The Integration of Desire* section 6.

For more about Gandhi's approach to resolving conflict, a useful source is Joan V. Bondurant, *Conquest of Violence.*

Types of integration

Water falling, sogging the earthlands,
weighting grasses, dripping melancholic
from the bowed needles.
Fear it not:
for it washes old leaves
and the cases of creatures,
all, from the tree's definition
to time's flow below.
The cloud's ceiling closes
one movement, one meaning:
whence the wind blows,
where the stream goes.

This is part of a long poem I wrote in Norway in 1985. The overwhelming theme of this poem was a celebration of what at that time, for lack of any better label, I called an experience of God. I would now generally prefer to call it an experience of the archetype of the integrated psyche or the God archetype. If one has a sense of the overwhelming meaningfulness of the world around, that meaning does not necessarily come from the world itself, but rather from the shape and structure of the experience. I wrote a good deal about God at that time, but I'm not sure that I ever really 'believed in' God.

Sometimes, in an attempt to fit into a group, I have rationalised "God" into something else that I experienced, and told myself that by joining in God-language I was really talking about this. This was the case when I got married in a Quaker meeting house and discovered that however open the Quaker way of doing things, the use of wedding vows involving God was non-negotiable. I told myself that this was just a way of giving the marriage a deeper meaning in the context of the community and went along with it, but in retrospect I think that was a wrong judgement. Having an experience of something that one might choose to call 'God' is one thing, but making a vow to God or before God is quite another, as it suggests that God is an agency, and that responsibility for the marriage is not just a matter for me, my partner and the surrounding community – as it unavoidably is.

How can one make sense of such an outlook: finding God acutely meaningful, and yet not believing in him? I think the Middle Way in which metaphysical claims are clearly rejected, together with the theory of embodied meaning, provide an alternative outlook in which such an outlook is no longer contradictory. The intellectual mistake that seems to be entrenched into our culture is to think of meaning in a way that is subjugated to belief – as though one needed to believe something first in order to find it meaningful. But our flesh and blood existence actually suggests the opposite. Meaning, whether of God or anything else, is a basic experience linked into our bodies. It is belief that may build on and follow meaning in some cases, not vice-versa. This also fits into a threefold structure in which desire is at the base, even before meaning arises.

The stacked Venn diagram here illustrates this structure. All beliefs are meanings, but not vice-versa, and all meanings are desires, but not vice-versa. Desires are the basic constituents of all these mental processes.

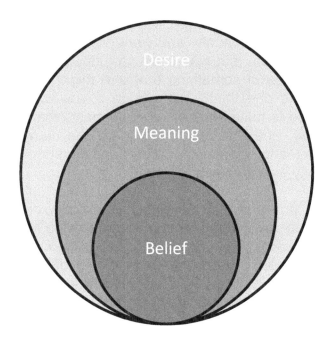

This structure may make more sense with some definitions. Such definitions are never final, but they aid clarity:

Desire is any energy, drive or motive that actually or potentially creates mental or physical activity, conscious or unconscious.

Meaning is the habitual attachment of desire to a symbol. A 'symbol' here can be any object we experience (e.g. a word, a picture, a tune) and associate with meaning.

Belief is a habitual motive of commitment to a particular pattern of meaningful symbols that are interpreted as representations (i.e. a cognitive model).

As you can see here, meaning is desire associated with symbols, whilst belief takes those symbols and forms them into accounts of what we think the world is like. We can be committed to those accounts to varying degrees, from a provisional theory or hypothesis to a rigid metaphysical belief.

Another way of understanding this progression between the three types of process is in terms of neural connections in the brain. The desire response is a very basic type of neural connection. For example, a sexual response needs little deliberate cultivation: it is 'hard-wired' into our brains. The associations that create a certain energy-response to symbols, however, need to be developed through active experience as we explore the world as young children. For example, as a child understands the meaning of the word 'in' in relation to boxes, houses, fields etc, a new neural connection is created and gradually strengthened. Beliefs consist in more complex sets of neural connections that arise in response to sets of symbols that represent the world for us. These could be the connections that lead me to believe that it is raining outside (in response to the noise of dripping and drumming), or that a tin of beans contains edible stuff, or that Ulan Bator is the capital of Mongolia. These connections are not just those that fit the symbols together, but also those that commit me to them as representations of how I think things are. At each level the symbols become more complex and more reliant on experience.

The more common pattern, in metaphysically-dominated thinking, is to understand meaning in terms of belief. In this view, meaning has to be propositional and explicit, only occurring in sentences. The huge proportion of our mental processes that occur unconsciously are excluded from either meaning or belief, and what makes a symbol meaningful is assumed to be its capacity to form a basis of belief. But much of what we find meaningful has nothing to do with belief: mythical beings, stories, works of art, and music are all examples of things that have a significance for us regardless of what we believe about them.

Some of that meaning, as Jung pointed out, is archetypal: it rouses desires within a basic psychic structure that we all share rather than from specific external experiences. For example, the Shadow archetype depends on an association with the rejected psyche beyond the ego, and we project this archetype onto people whom we regard as evil. The meaning of an archetype has nothing to do with our beliefs, but involves a much more basic pattern of meaningfulness than comes with our embodied existence. Fear of the devil resonates in our bodies whether or not we "believe in" the devil. Similarly, the archetypal meaning of God can be understood as a forward projection of ourselves as entirely integrated. The world appears – indeed is – unified and meaningful, because the barriers between the desires that we have in relation to it have been at least temporarily removed. We can celebrate this religious experience just as much – if not more so – when we recognise it as just that – an experience – than if we place it within a metaphysical structure of belief that we then have to defend.

The vast majority of our desires, meanings and beliefs are unconscious or pre-conscious. They consist of successive layers of association and response with increasing complexity, building up to conscious representations as the tip of the iceberg rather than the base. Because all three layers are based on energies, those energies can be opposed to one another or they can be integrated. That means that not only desires, but also meanings and beliefs, can be integrated. We need to develop integration of all three inter-dependent types in order to make lasting progress with integration in general.

Summary
- Belief is developed in dependence on meaning, not the other way round, because of the embodied nature of meaning
- If we see belief as dependent on meaning, we are in a better position to understand archetypal meaning without metaphysical assumptions
- Meaning is in turn developed in dependence on desire, as energy needs to be attached to a symbol for it to be meaningful
- This model can also be understood in terms of the strength and complexity of neural connections

Further Reading
The three types of integration are discussed in *Middle Way Philosophy 1: The Path of Objectivity* 6.g, with each type of integration then providing the theme of each of the other volumes of the *Middle Way Philosophy* series. The implications of this for religion are discussed in *Truth on the Edge* chapter 8.

The poem can be found in my published collection *North Cape.*

More on Jung's archetypes can be found in *The Archetypes and the Collective Unconscious* and *Aion.*

4. Practical Application

Integrating theory and practice

I have recently been reading the extraordinary book *Antifragile* by Nassim Nicholas Taleb. Taleb's book is a passionate argument for the need to take into account extreme events that are beyond the range of normal estimations of probability, and not to base our judgements on an idea of normality that is actually fragile – i.e. subject to rare but catastrophic destruction. He is extremely critical of the dogmatic reliance on theory that takes itself to be all-encompassing. Instead, he has a conservative respect for traditions that have been built up through centuries of trial and error and adapted themselves to abnormal as well as normal conditions.

Taleb presents evidence that in many cases, the contribution of theory towards practical advances has been greatly overestimated. Doctors who work by trial and error are dismissed as 'quacks', but he maintains that most drugs have been developed by a trial and error process, and the use of big theory to develop medical treatments has often given rise to larger negative side effects. Key technological advances, such as the steam engine and the jet engine, have been made by relatively uneducated tinkerers. However, it is those with academic posts who often tell a dominant story that overestimates the role of theory. As Yogi Berra put it, "In theory there is no difference between theory and practice; in practice there is."

Taleb offers a helpful rebalancing of the perspective, but he also admits that theory plays a role. Since, in a wider sense, we all make use of theories all the time, it could hardly be otherwise. Theory can be understood in the most basic sense as a belief on the basis of which we act. When a primitive hunter, depending on the experience of previous years, gets together a hunting party to take advantage of an animal migration that is likely to be happening in the next valley, he is offering a theory that the migration happens every year at that time, and acting on that basis. Without any such action, the theory would be no more than a speculation, but on the other hand a hunting party that set off at a random time of year to a random place, without any such guiding theory, would be much more likely to return empty handed.

Theory without practice is dogma. Practice without theory is random guesswork. In some ways random guesswork can be more effective than dogma (at least it is not systematically deluded), but an interactive balance is even better. In order to act we have to have a framework of beliefs to act in, and theory just makes that framework of beliefs more systematic. On the other hand, to make progress in objectivity, theory must subject itself to the challenges of potentially disconfirmatory trials in active experience. Without that challenge, theory is very much subject to the delusion that it has the whole picture.

The odd thing about 'practice' in general is that it thrives on this disconfirmation. You would not call a footballer a good player who could only score goals against one opposing team, but none of the others. Likewise, genuine practice encounters a variety of testing circumstances. Meditators test the strength of their practice, not by retreating for such lengthy periods that the retreat becomes an end in itself, but by putting themselves in difficult situations in which their mindfulness is tested. The more testing your practice, over the longer-term, the more adequate your theory.

So, the practice of Middle Way Philosophy is not just a one-way process in which a comprehensive theory is applied, but a feedback loop in which practice helps to adjust theory. Feedback loops can be of two kinds: positive and negative.

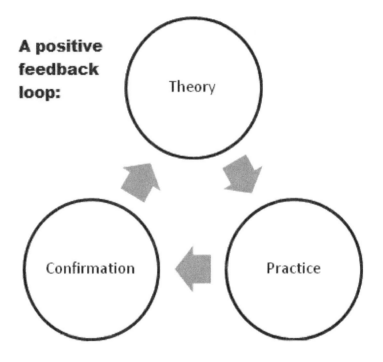

A positive feedback loop:

In the case of a positive feedback loop, practice in accordance with the belief you started with fulfils your goals and confirms the theory. This provides confidence in the theory, but does not help you to improve it. In the case of a negative feedback loop, however, more is learned, because by practising the theory and finding

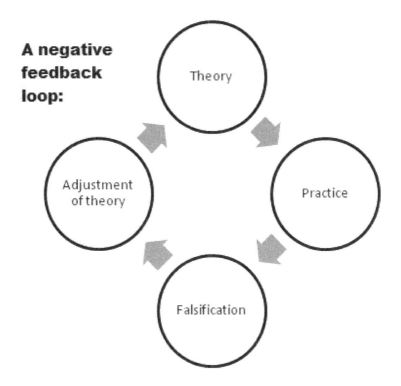

A negative feedback loop:

Theory

Practice

Falsification

Adjustment of theory

that it does not fulfill your goals you are obliged to adjust the theory.

What we learn through practice, then, is sustainable and resilient in a way that theory by itself is not. When theory dominates practice, it leads to confirmation bias, as we place ourselves in practical situations that fit the theory, and at the same time put off the eventual disastrous collapse of a long-held theory. When practice dominates theory, on the other hand, we are more likely to genuinely test the theory in a variety of conditions. When the theory is "falsified" (or at least, found wanting), this is not a conclusive proof that the theory is wrong, but it does give us a good reason for adjusting the theory and comparing it with other alternatives. Each time we are wrong, our wisdom improves a little.

However, the variety of circumstances that need to be met by a practice are not only external. Much of what determines the appropriateness of a practice is its relationship to your mental states. Is it the right practice for you, now? Meditation is one of the most direct ways of practising the Middle Way, but some people are not ready to practice meditation until they have gained a basic level of psychological integration that provides them with enough confidence to do the practice. The basic grounds of confidence are needed in any practice before a cutting edge of challenge can begin to shape an adequate approach. In developing this basic confidence we are often dependent on teachers and mentors.

In the remainder of this section I will explore a selection of key practices that can be applications of the Middle Way. The practices covered here will be far from exhaustive. However, what does seem clear is that practice of some kind is essential for the Middle Way. A merely theoretical perspective is productive only of complacent adherence to metaphysical models. However, the key element of what we need to understand as "practical" is not necessarily bodily movement or acquired skill – rather, it is the ability to test out our models in a variety of new experienced circumstances. This can sometimes extend the "practical" into unexpected areas that might otherwise be mistaken for theory.

Summary

- Theory is always dependent on practice for its objectivity, as practice is required to test out a theory and make it adequate to conditions (or antifragile)
- Practice is also dependent on theory, as all actions take place in an assumed representation of the context
- The practice of Middle Way Philosophy subjects the theory to negative feedback loops, although positive ones can also be helpful to provide confidence
- Practice thus needs to be selected by what will best improve our adequacy, but also depending on what we are ready for.

Further Reading

There is an overall survey of integrative practice in *Truth on the Edge* chapter 5. Feedback loops are also discussed in *Middle Way Philosophy 1: The Path of Objectivity* 3.e.

On the concept of antifragility as adequacy to a wide range of conditions encountered in practice, Nassim Nicholas Taleb's *Antifragile* is highly recommended.

Meditation

I have already discussed meditation, beginning with some of my own practical experience, in 'how integration works'. There I suggested that meditation is a good way of getting to grips directly with both the Middle Way and integration. Meditation practice has a tendency to make us aware of our own relative lack of integration almost immediately, and it is flexibility in responding to the mental conditions we encounter that is important, avoiding fixed (metaphysical) beliefs about the practice.

Here, however, I will say a bit more about the practical judgements involved in beginning meditation. I will assume no prior knowledge or experience. Seasoned meditators may thus prefer to skip the rest of this chapter.

To start meditation you will need two main things: a physical posture, and sufficient knowledge of a practice. Both of these are best discussed and developed in the context of a meditation class, in live interaction with an experienced meditator. What I can say here can offer little more than some initial pointers.

The importance of your posture should not be underestimated, as meditation is something you do with your body. Yes, it is possible to meditate in any position, but some positions are much easier to maintain awareness in than others. If you are standing, it is harder to relax your body, and if you are moving around you will need to give some attention to directing yourself and avoiding obstacles. At the other extreme, if you are lying down, or slouched on a sofa, it will probably be difficult to maintain awareness, and you will get sleepy quite quickly. The first practical application of the Middle Way, here, then, is physical. You need to achieve an alert posture that is compatible with the physical relaxation that will also be necessary in meditation, avoiding the fixed beliefs either just that your body should relax or that it should just be alert, but rather maximally combining the two.

The type of posture this balance should ideally result in will be upright, with the spine straightened upwards but not rigid. A kneeling posture can usually do this best, but sitting on an upright stool or chair is a possible alternative.

Knowledge of a practice is necessary to provide an initial framework to guide what you do whilst meditating. Initially it may be necessary to be quite rigid in using a particular "practice", in order to get a sense of how to meditate, just as when learning to drive you at first need to just do exactly what the instructor says. When you get an experiential sense of how to meditate, you may be able to evolve your own "practice".

Here, then, is another aspect of the Middle Way applied to meditation. Just as we always need theories to act in any other context, meditation is no exception. At first, in this unfamiliar practical environment, you will probably be wise to cling closely to the framework that brought you there. However, if you continue to do so, it is likely to constrain your experience of that environment. Meditation practices need to be held provisionally, just like any other theory, but nevertheless you will need to learn a specific practice to provide scaffolding for your future progress.

In many ways, it doesn't matter which practice you choose, as long as you do it in a regular way. However, there are many advantages to starting with a simple practice, and one that does not carry a lot of cultural baggage. If you start off by visualising Tibetan deities (unless you are culturally Tibetan), you might end up quite quickly alienated. If a practice is complex, that can also make it harder to master, and create a distraction from the practice itself. Two simple practices that I can recommend are from the Buddhist tradition: mindfulness of breathing (also known as anapana sati) and just sitting (also known as zazen).

In the mindfulness of breathing, one aims to connect with the meaningfulness of a basic physical experience: the breath. This is something close to the basic 'felt sense' of embodied meaning. The amazing thing about the breath is that, like a beautiful sunset or pattern in the sand, it has its own intrinsic, non-obsessive interest. By becoming absorbed in an interest in the breath, we will find our body relaxing and mental states integrating. It can engage the right hemisphere of the brain rather than the left, and in the process provide some basic conditions for competing desires of the left brain to integrate.

'Just sitting' may sound undemanding, but this is not the case. When just sitting it is even more important to start off with a balanced posture and with a base of awareness in your body. The idea then is to simply observe what happens in your mind and let go of it, not pursuing chains of obsessive left-hemisphere thought, but always allowing thoughts to take their place in a wider context of awareness.

A third application of the Middle Way in meditation involves the degree of wilful effort you put into the practice. If you only focus narrowly on the object of concentration, you will just be repressing other desires.

The whole point of meditation is to be aware of competing desires and to gently integrate them into the meditation. On the other hand, if you exert no effort at all, you will just enter a distracted state and may as well not have meditated. A consistent thread of intention to meditate needs to be present, but on the other hand you need to be open enough to allow potential distractions to appear and then be nudged into the practice.

Whatever practice you do, it is not an instant panacea to all your problems: more likely a balancing function in your life. It will be more effective if you are committed to it, but it may also need to take its place alongside other useful practices. If you learn with a live meditation teacher, and approach it committedly but realistically, it can be a central way of engaging with the Middle Way in practice.

The three types of balancing that I have outlined can also be applied to many other activities. For example, 'physical' activities such as yoga or Tai Ch'i can be seen as merely more active versions of meditation: ones that may be essential towards an integrating recognition of the basic role that embodied experience plays in our awareness.

Summary
- The Middle Way can be practised through at least three different balancing processes in meditation
- Meditation requires a founding basis of balance in posture, between tension and relaxation
- A further balance in meditation practice lies between adherence to a specific "practice" and responding flexibly and directly to your own experience

- A third balancing element in meditation is the balance between wilful effort and open relaxation. Continuity of attention needs to be combined with relaxation.

Further Reading

I have written about balanced effort in *Middle Way Philosophy 2: The Integration of Desire* 4.a and about meditation in the same book 4.f. I hope that over time the Middle Way Society will develop a distinctive approach to meditation that stresses the Middle Way, and develop further resources.

There are many introductions to meditation around, from different traditions of practice. My own experience of meditation has been through the Buddhist tradition, specifically in the way taught by what is now called the Triratna Buddhist Community. A particularly useful book in this tradition is Kamalashila's *Meditation: The Buddhist Way of Tranquillity and Insight.* Online resources in this tradition are also offered by *Wildmind* at **www.wildmind.org** .

Critical Thinking

Critical Thinking is something that I have learned by teaching it: but there are few better ways to learn something than to teach it. When I arrived back in a sixth form college teaching job, after four years out studying for my Ph.D. and being immersed in Philosophy, I found that the college was involved in a pilot for a new qualification in Critical Thinking. Teaching Critical Thinking allowed me to teach a much wider range of students than I would have encountered teaching Philosophy – for it consists in the skills long prized by Philosophy, but applied in every area of life.

These skills are the skills of argument. Argument is all around us every day. We meet it in conversation, in newspapers, on TV and radio, and in the study of almost any subject. Whenever we make some kind of claim, and attempt to justify that claim by giving reasons to support it, we are using argument. It might be something as simple and everyday as "I suggest you put a lid on that saucepan because it will boil quicker" or "Manchester United are going to be relegated this season. You can see how badly they've been doing."

Why should I put a lid on the saucepan? The assertion that I should is backed up with a reason – that it will boil quicker. Is this a good reason? It could be further justified from experience, or alternatively by appealing to laws of physics concerning changes in temperature and the effect of air convection in slowing heating. It's also relevant to the conclusion, though it assumes that I want the saucepan to boil quicker: maybe I don't, or maybe I want to keep the lid off for some other reason. Studying critical thinking helps one to become very clear about simple examples like this, and then go on to use the same skills on more complex arguments. This is often seen as being primarily the skill of reasoning, and sometimes people do use reasons to support their claims that aren't completely relevant in supporting them, though we wrongly assume that they are. However, more important in Critical Thinking generally is the awareness of the assumptions we are making, and the way we focus our awareness on those assumptions.

The development of critical thinking is crucial to the practice of the Middle Way. The Middle Way enables us to address conditions by avoiding the interpretation of our experience through metaphysical preconceptions. Very often those preconceptions become apparent through critical thinking as unjustified assumptions. We need a certain amount of awareness to become aware of a critical problem and apply thought to it, but critical thinking skills are then needed to identify what the unhelpful and unjustified assumptions are.

Here is a simple example of an unjustified metaphysical assumption having an immediate impact and reducing moral awareness. Fred is a committed anti-fox hunting saboteur. Bill is a friend of Fred who does not have strong views on the hunting issue, but Fred persuades him to come along to the meeting of his anti-hunting campaign group one day. Bill has an open mind and starts asking some difficult questions about the justification of direct action to disrupt hunting. Fred takes this as a personal attack and instead of discussing the issues he raised, has a row with Bill after the meeting. The friendship between the two subsequently ends.

Fred's implicit reasoning goes something like this:
1. Fox hunting is absolutely wrong

2. Disrupting fox hunting must thus be right

3. Bill has questioned the justification of disrupting hunts

4. Therefore, Bill must be wrong.

Here, he has assumed that if fox-hunting is wrong, it must be right to disrupt it, which is not necessarily the case. Fox hunting could consistently be wrong and yet it be wrong to disrupt it – for example, because it is too dangerous and either the saboteurs or the hunters might be injured. Fred could have quite consistently continued to believe that fox hunting was wrong and yet considered the criticisms. Bill could also have been doing the campaign group a favour by asking questions that might challenge it to improve the justification of its campaigning tactics.

Fred's response, is, of course, a negative emotional reaction, and it could be considered and dealt with on that level. If Fred had simply been more aware he might also have been able to avoid this response. However, he also made a mistake which could have been identified in terms of critical thinking, which is that of assuming that (2) was true because (1) was true.

However, Fred also made an absolute and metaphysical assumption in his belief that fox hunting is absolutely wrong, rather than being merely provisionally so. Given that no absolute truths can be gained through experience, in believing that the party's policy is absolutely correct, Fred was adopting an absolute moral position on a dogmatic basis that goes beyond experience.

This tendency towards specific types of unrecognised metaphysical assumption is understood in psychological terms as *cognitive bias*. There are a number of identifiable patterns to the kinds of mistakes

of reasoning that we make. There are a great many different cognitive biases, but one of the most common is *confirmation bias*, which we have already discussed –

this is the tendency to focus only on evidence that confirms your theory. In this case, Fred is only interested in discussing ideas that confirm his beliefs about fox hunting and how to combat it, and rules out challenges from consideration. Critical Thinking is a kind of self-administered therapy against cognitive biases.

But let's try to think about Fred's position with as much incrementality as possible. Even if Fred had not questioned his assumption that fox hunting is absolutely wrong, he would still be making progress if he had avoided assuming disrupting fox hunting might thus be right, and been open to discussing Bill's questions. Thus those who are committed to metaphysical ideas can still practise critical thinking to a limited degree, and thus be less dogmatic than they would have been otherwise.

For example, it would be possible to do some critical thinking whilst being a devout Roman Catholic and accepting the Pope's authority. One could have the rigour of the Jesuits. However, the impossibility of questioning the founding dogma would continue to create strains in that critical thinking by imposing no-go areas. The same impulses towards widening awareness and open questioning that lead to critical thinking are also very likely to lead one into philosophical questions, and to the further dismantling of dogma.

Nevertheless, critical thinking is a good place to start, especially for the many people who are not yet ready to face up to the dogmas in their lives philosophically. Anyone who studies and practises critical thinking is in effect beginning to practise the Middle Way and to address conditions more fully than they did before.

Summary

- Critical Thinking is the skill of analysing and evaluating argument, which is used constantly all around us
- Critical Thinking is very useful in checking the coherence of beliefs via the justification of the arguments supporting them
- This can also help to make us aware of metaphysical beliefs, and to overcome cognitive biases, thus avoiding metaphysics and following the Middle Way

Further Reading

There are lots of good introductions to Critical Thinking available. Some recommended ones are *Critical Reasoning: A Practical Introduction* by Anne Thomson and *Critical Thinking* by Brooke Noel Moore and Richard Parker.

The Arts

The arts have been central to my experience from an early age. At the age of seven I started learning classical piano, and, with only occasional gaps, have been playing ever since, often with a romantic intensity that shows its role as a rebalancing function for me. I love Beethoven sonatas, and am prone to underestimating the difficulties of playing them well in my haste to master them. I engage with music very much with my right brain and have very little head for musical theory, despite my love of theory in other areas.

Music is perhaps the art that relates most directly to embodied experience, and embodied experience encompasses both 'reason' and 'emotion'. The rhythms of music are meaningful to us because of their relationship to our heartbeat and pulse. The movement away from the dominant 'home' key (in Western music) and back to it in the final cadence of a piece reflects a physical tension and relaxation in our bodies. Melody relates to our physical experience of vocalisation, with the tones of voices being more basic to our experience of them than the words.

The other art with which I have been engaged from an early age is creative writing and literature. Thanks to an inspiring sixth form English teacher, I gained a place at Cambridge to study English. Again, my love of literature and writing is very much coloured by romanticism. What I sought in it was moments of insight, metaphorical connection, or rapture. I aspired to be a poet long before I became interested in philosophy, and I still often feel that the philosopher is filtered through a more deeply-rooted poet. However, I changed subject after my first year at Cambridge due to frustration with the study of literature as an end in itself. For me it needs to take its place within a larger framework of thought.

Literature appeals less directly to our embodied sense than music, but on the other hand can unify metaphorical constructions that have been built up from our image schemas. Poetry (or at least, the best poetry) does this through metaphor. For example, in his poem 'The Wild Swans at Coole', W.B. Yeats brings together his experience of the swans on the lake and his own feelings of sadness at the loss of past youth and love. It is neither a poem just 'about' swans, nor is it a poem just 'about' Yeats' emotions, but rather about the relationship between the two. It is the connection between the two that communicates the meaning of both the swans and Yeats' emotions more powerfully to us.

I have no skill in the visual arts, but much appreciation of them. What I often seek most in paintings, particularly, is the sating of a sort of hunger for visual representations of *archetypes*. I find these most often in Renaissance painting, with its Greek gods, heroes, saints and bible stories. In the Renaissance, as McGilchrist comments, there seems to have been an increase in the direct contact between the hemispheres – at least in those culturally dominant. Our psychic functions, if the art is anything to go by, were then more easily embodied rather than reduced to concepts.

The visual arts also make a direct impact on our physical experience through colour and form, whether that form is three or four dimensional. The work of art is not just important to us because of the concepts or feelings it expresses, but because of the impact it makes on our bodies through visual experience. This impact is perhaps most striking in film, and at its greatest in an IMAX cinema that fills our visual field and makes us feel that we are 'actually there' having the physical experience that is being depicted: even though that experience is only being communicated to us through our visual field.

Whichever arts one chooses to focus on, the integrative functions of either creating or appreciating them are similar. In any arts we are using symbols that relate directly to our embodied experience, often ones that relate more directly to that experience than the conceptual language we can only develop in sole dependence on a particular metaphor. By relating our conceptual ideas to that basic physical experience, we are in a better position to integrate those ideas, just as we are in meditation.

Our meanings are *fragmented* in the same way that desires can be in conflict with each other. Given that we associate symbols with our desires, conflicts between desires (like that between the two mules) can often be seen alternatively as conflicts between different symbols that we identify with. Those symbols are likely to be embedded in a language. In some cases we do not understand a language that we take to be alien, whilst in others we do not wish to engage with it. In most cases there is a combination of the two. Imagine the two mules as the French and the Germans, or as a desire to stop smoking competing with a desire to continue smoking. The two sides need a basic understanding with each other, and a basic engagement with what each other means, before they can reach agreement to alter their model of the situation to mutual benefit. The arts help enormously with the integration of meaning that is required to create this basic understanding.

There are three specific kinds of ways that the arts can support integration of meaning. Of these, the last seems the most important and the most specific to the arts, but the others also play a role.

- Adding to the fund of symbols
- Clarifying symbols within a cognitive model
- Linking cognitive models through ambiguity

When the arts add to the fund of symbols, they just provide new possibilities for symbols that can be associated with our physical experience and thus made meaningful. This comes particularly through appreciation of the arts. I read a book and learn new vocabulary. I go to the gallery and absorb the possibility of new modes of visual expression and new imaginative forms. I listen to music and add to the fund of possible forms of musical expression. The more impression this art makes on me, the more likely I am to use these symbols subsequently.

Adding to the fund of symbols just makes more meaning-resources available to me. It does not necessarily mean that I will use those resources, or that I will use them very effectively. I could be a walking dictionary and yet lack creativity or practical application for these resources. Yet nevertheless, a fund of meaningful symbols is a necessary condition for being able to use them meaningfully.

The arts also help us to clarify symbols within a cognitive model. If I read more literature, I can develop a stronger and more precise sense of the meaning of words, and of the different ways they have been (or might be) used. If I write creatively, I can also even create and stipulate new words: but the more I use them, the better defined and more useful they become. The more I practice the piano, the better my precision of playing, dynamics and tone can become – so my use of musical symbols becomes clearer. However, the arts perhaps play a subsidiary role here compared to critical thinking, which places a premium on this kind of clarification. This function tends to comprise the more technical and critical side of the arts.

However, it is still important to use symbols with clarity. Without such clarity it is much more difficult to form beliefs that are adequate to the circumstances. Clarity in an art such as the classical piano tradition is liable to become a bit of an end in itself, but it still provides valuable practice in creating a coherent form that is fully meaningful to ourselves and others. That coherence becomes most important when we have to translate it into decisive action. Developing clarity within the framework offered by a particular artistic tradition can be seen as a more physically-engaged dry run for other complex judgements, such as deciding whether to trust a financial offer, what house to buy, or which philosophy to adopt.

The most important way that the arts integrate, however, is through ambiguity. In all of the arts, the use of more basic and physically embodied forms of expression, and the use of metaphor, can bring us back to an ambiguous base line that can help to stop us getting too entrenched in a particular cognitive model. Most of the way we think involves taking a particular cognitive model – that is, a dried out and extended metaphor – for granted. It is only when that model conflicts with conditions, and thus confronts us with its inadequacy, that we might be reminded that it is only based on a metaphor.

When everything that we have built on a particular metaphor suddenly crumbles, we can avoid total collapse by avoiding a total investment of meaning into that one metaphor. We are better able to switch and develop new metaphorical models if we can go back to the basic physical ground of ambiguity from which those models emerged. This is the experience of image schemas by which we relate experience to symbols from early infancy, and from which we extend metaphors, as discussed in 'embodied meaning' above. The arts constantly remind us of that ambiguity, whether through the ambiguous forms of art, the metaphorical openness of poetry, or the ultimate ambiguity of music.

One area of the arts that particularly trades on ambiguity is humour. We experience pleasure when two

cognitive models collide, and our tendency to take the cognitive model to be ultimate is briefly challenged. For example, the panda that "eats shoots and leaves", that we place in the framework of wildlife and its predictable behaviour, suddenly becomes an anthropomorphised gun-toting creature when pronounced as though there was a comma after "eats". We experience pleasure as the dead metaphor is suddenly connected to the right hemisphere and becomes live again, and our meaning connections become slightly fuller.

Apart from the sheer delight that they give us, then, the arts are an ultimate insurance policy against disaster. If your sense of meaning resides, not in particular cognitive models (important though these are for practical reasons), but in physical sense and metaphor, then the collapse of your theory will be no more of an ultimate problem than the collapse of your house. As long as you have the land for the foundations (your physical experience) and the construction materials (metaphor), you will always be able to rebuild.

Summary
- All the arts are meaningful to us because of their relationship to physical experience, either directly or through metaphor
- Meaning can be fragmented when associated desires are in conflict
- Integration of meaning is required for integration of belief that is based on it
- Integration of meaning can be developed through the arts by adding to the fund of symbols, clarifying symbols and (most importantly) linking cognitive models through ambiguity
- Integration of meaning supports the Middle Way by preventing us from getting too entrenched in the

cognitive models that are assumed by metaphysical beliefs

Further Reading

There is a detailed discussion of the process and practice of integrating meaning in *Middle Way Philosophy 3: The Integration of Meaning* sections 5 and 6.

Mark Johnson's *The Meaning of the Body* Part 3 discusses the relationship of the arts to embodied meaning.

Integrative therapies

A therapy is generally understood as a treatment or practice within a medical model: that is, to cure a disease or other mental or physical problem. The classic medical model includes a diagnosis, prescription and treatment of some kind. Psychotherapies may stick closely to that medical model in some cases, or in others stretch it beyond its original boundaries, but they tend to remain rooted in it.

The medical model has definite limitations, because its prescriptions (whether of drugs or other treatments) tend to lock us into a particular cognitive model. The disease is diagnosed, in the process creating an adversary and pathologising a condition that might not previously have been understood in those terms. Whereas previously there was me, now there is me and a threatening parasitic 'disease' separate from me that needs to be combated. A prescription is offered that has only a certain probability of success, because of the complexity of the human system which means that the treatment is sometimes worse than the disease. The prescription aims at a state of 'health' that again often over-simplifies our experience, as it may fall well short of greater moral or spiritual goals for human life.

Nevertheless, the idea of an integrative therapy is not a contradiction in terms. What we may regard as 'disease' is sometimes attributable to particularly rigid beliefs and lack of integration. Therapies developed in a medical model may particularly help people to alleviate some extremely disintegrated states. Although due to the widespread false distinction between scientific fact and moral value, very few therapists are willing to define their work in moral terms, many also do stretch the idea of therapy into a wider scheme of 'personal growth'. In some ways 'personal growth' has acted as a proxy ethics for many in modern times.

Such therapies may involve drugs, 'talking cures', or practices that include elements of meditation. If someone has schizophrenia, for example, they are in a profoundly disintegrated state that may require treatment with drugs before it is possible to even engage with any other integrative practice. However, the drawbacks of dependency and side effects that tend to go with drug therapies are well known. One could see medical use of drugs as primarily helping to create a starting point in extreme cases of mental illness, rather than being a form of practice in themselves. So at other levels we are left with talking cures and personal practices

Psychoanalysis is the 'talking cure' that began in a medical model, even if its effectiveness within that model has often been questioned, and it is through Freud and Jung's practice of psychoanalysis that the integrative model was first developed. However, in the century or so since Freud, a whole host of types of psychotherapy and cognitive therapy have developed. The following list is unlikely to be complete, but tries to identify some of the main types and sub-types:

- Psychosynthesis
- Adlerian therapy
- Freudian Psychoanalysis
- Jungian Psychoanalysis
  - Depth psychology
  - Process oriented psychotherapy
  - Transpersonal psychology
- Humanistic Psychology
  - Focusing
  - Primal integration

- Gestalt therapy
- Specific practical techniques
  - Hypnotherapy
  - Drama therapy
  - Dance therapy
  - Art therapy
  - Play therapy
  - Horticultural therapy
- Cognitive behavioural therapy
  - Schema based therapy
  - Acceptance and commitment therapy
- Body psychotherapy (Reichian)
  - Biofeedback
  - Encounter groups
  - Emotionally focused therapy
- Buddhist-influenced psychotherapies
  - Contemplative psychotherapy
  - Core process psychotherapy
  - Dialectical behaviour therapy
  - Mindfulness-based cognitive therapy
  - Mindfulness-based stress reduction
- Rational emotive behaviour therapy
- Systemic therapy
- Transactional analysis
- Nonviolent communication
- Counselling

Up to a point, any of these different forms of therapy might aid integration. Many of them are geared more towards dealing with what has been identified as 'mental illness', whether in the extreme form of psychosis or neurosis, than in aiding moral or spiritual progress beyond this point. This therapeutic limitation might take the form of a course of treatment after which the patient is considered 'cured'. However, there are also some therapies here that are more open-ended and can support integration beyond this point. These therapies tend to work in a basically dialectical and integrative way, in which the experiences of the patient and the therapist enter into conversation to help the patient gradually move beyond the limitations of previous identifications, meanings or beliefs. Non-violent communication is a strong example of this, as it applies dialogical therapeutic methods to resolving all kinds of conflicts in a much wider social context.

I will focus here in a bit more detail on just a few examples from the above list.

Transpersonal psychology is directly oriented to breaking out of the limitations of the medical model, without excluding the domain of traditional psychology. It is flexible about the models it uses, drawing on both Jungian and humanistic models.

Jungian psychotherapy is likely to be particularly focused on working with unconscious elements of experience, so will include discussion of dreams and other ways that archetypes enter experience. This can aid the integration of repressed unconscious elements of the psyche. It may be more useful outside the medical model than within it.

Focusing is a specific practice developed by Eugene Gendlin, and can be done either alone or with a mentor. It helps us to get in touch with our 'felt sense' or basic experience of meaning, and thus with ideas and concerns that would otherwise not be articulated.

Cognitive behavioural therapy (CBT) works with our limiting assumptions and the unhelpful behaviours that arise from them. A range of cognitive biases have been identified that interfere with the integration of our beliefs, and CBT works to reduce these biases, particularly through reflection and discourse. This can be particularly helpful in the treatment of acute depression.

Mindfulness-based stress reduction (MBSR) is in fact meditation done in a therapeutic setting, focusing particularly on the ways that meditation can help with pain management

Mindfulness-based cognitive therapy combines elements of MBSR and CBT to help prevent relapses for those prone to depression.

The choice of therapies, and whether you use them at all, depends very much on your personal situation. If you are struggling to engage with any other integrative practices, and your life feels too much out of control, the right therapy might help you to reach a better point of departure for your own integrative path. Even if you can engage with other integrative practices, such as meditation, critical thinking, or the arts, some therapies that are not too much limited by the medical model might provide a parallel aspect of practice offering an alternative perspective.

It is important, however, not to see the whole of the practice of the Middle Way within the framework of therapies. Despite the ways that they can sometimes transcend the medical model, most therapies remain rooted in it. This medical model tends to include ethics only in a subsidiary and conventionalised form ("ethics" is seen as an aspect of therapy rather than the other way round). A 'moral therapy' that fully questions the fact-value distinction and thus applies the integration model to all our judgements has yet to emerge, and if it did perhaps it would have gone beyond the whole sphere of therapy.

If you see Middle Way Philosophy as another form of therapy, it will appear to be a redundant further addition to the list. Instead it offers an overall rationale that can include therapies. The analysis of desire, meaning and belief can also show much of the relationship between different forms of therapy: for example, Jungian approaches work primarily with desires, Focusing primarily with meaning, and Cognitive Behavioural Therapy with beliefs. These different forms of therapy are likely to be more useful in addressing different conditions because of the different ways they seek to integrate.

Summary
- There are a wide range of therapies which may be of use in integrative practice, particularly in dealing with basic internal conflicts that prevent us from beginning to engage with other integrative practices
- Most therapies are constrained by, or at least rooted in, a medical model
- Middle Way Philosophy is particularly distinguished from any therapy in the sense that moral objectivity is part of its basic model

Further Reading
A wide range of literature and online resources are offered by the different types of therapies listed above. These are too voluminous to be listed here, but an online search for the therapy concerned should lead you to helpful resources. A useful online guide to the different types of psychotherapy is provided by the UK Council for Psychotherapy at **http://www.psychotherapy.org.uk/different_types_of _psychotherapy.html** .

Ethical practice

Back in 1985, I was a young student taking a gap year before going to university. I spent some of that time working on a pig farm in Norway. It had an intensive unit in the bottom of a spectacular valley, but the pigs very rarely got out of their cramped quarters to enjoy the clear air. Every morning I had to muck out the pigs. Once or twice during my stay, the slaughterhouse lorry came to pick up a load of pigs.

Just after one of these visits from the slaughterhouse lorry, I was talking to the farmer (a friendly young man), and asked him how he felt at saying farewell to the pigs he had reared from birth. "Nothing." He laughed, "Just money!" Then he contradicted himself "No, of course I feel something. It's sad. But it has to happen".

As I look back on this conversation now, it seems a clear example of the relationship between ethical practice and integration. The farmer was a pleasant chap, but in order to stay in the pig business it seemed clear that he had to repress some of his feelings – specifically those that maintained sympathy with the pigs who were on their way to being turned into bacon after being factory farmed. Given the lack of necessity for the product being produced (nobody really needs bacon), which produces an obvious belief that the pig industry is wrong, this belief and its associated desires have to be repressed in order to continue with the business.

I think that it was probably shortly after this conversation that I took one of the important moral decisions of my life – to become a vegetarian as soon as I left the farm. Soon afterwards I also went on to become a vegan. This was a moral practice because it required a moral effort: changing my eating habits, explaining to my parents, and making a fuss in restaurants. It would not particularly be a practice if everyone around me was a vegetarian, but an autonomous decision to differ from the community introduces moral effort. It's a practice I have kept up ever since, although the longer you do it, the easier it gets.

In the 'moral objectivity' chapter above I have already discussed some of the issues involved in making moral judgements. There I suggested that moral judgements are no different from other judgements, and that they are justified not just by coherence, but also by awareness of fallibility. If we were not aware of the fallibility of the moral assumptions that predominate in our society, we would never address those repressed beliefs that may be offering us a better way.

In the case of vegetarianism, my judgement is that this is straightforward. Though I don't want to be diverted here by a detailed argument on this topic, here is why in brief. Once you start using a cognitive model that is not just based on a very selective and now outdated account of human nutrition, or on convention, or on taste preferences which have largely just developed because of those social conventions, eating meat makes little sense. Not only does it involve widespread unnecessary suffering for animals, but also highly inefficient use of land, water and energy. It seems much more common for people in the West today to reject vegetarianism because of dogmatic assumptions that limit their thinking than it is for people to maintain vegetarianism dogmatically, because it is the vegetarians that are generally opening critical questions and addressing conditions that others are ignoring.

robertupeksa   27 apr 14, 11:26 AM

In this particular case, then, I think that improving my moral practice involved taking into account the consequences of my actions more fully. However, to take into account these consequences on a regular basis I needed to adopt a principle. There might be other people in other situations for whom overcoming a lifetime's rigid devotion to vegetarianism was actually a progressive move – though I'd suggest that even for them, just overcoming the rigidity by a little transgression would be better than eating huge amounts of meat. Ethical practice means, not doing a 'right thing' defined abstractly in a way beyond all experience, but moving forward from wherever you start.

Other ways of moving forward in ethical practice might involve long-term thinking about one's own habitual states, and an attempt to work on them in some depth: in other words to become virtuous. This is what might be described as virtue ethics thinking. In some cases one might need to invest more in one's own future capacity to make better judgements, rather than making choices that might be more obviously objective in other ways, such as leading to better consequences in the short-term.

I think some of the best decisions I have made of this sort have involved going on retreat. Primarily in the early years this meant going on Buddhist retreats where I was able to deepen my practice of meditation, or develop a variety of friendships that stimulated or supported me beyond my usual range of acquaintances. Even when my daughter was very young I went on retreat, and so did my wife – just not at the same time.

At other times, ethical practice might involve careful observation of one's own behaviour and mental states, and the decision to adopt a principle (what Buddhists would call a 'precept') to help one work more effectively with a particular condition. This might be about something much smaller than going vegetarian. For example, recently I noticed that if I checked email and went onto the internet too early in the morning, I could quickly get into a rather scattered state of mind in which I did not get on with writing and other important tasks in a concentrated way. I thus made myself a principle to start the day with meditation, reading and writing and put off checking email or going on the internet for at least a couple of hours. This has worked well. By the time I start to engage with the more fractured and disparate internet world, with one matter quickly following another, I feel I have already done some solid and productive work.

Of course (as discussed in the moral objectivity chapter above) this principle does not have to be adhered to with too much rigidity. It is more of the long-term reminder of an intention, a way of bringing a little more integration into my daily experience. However, there may be some days when there is some particular reason for engaging with important emails early on. It is also very specific to my situation. There are many moral principles that we can use like that: they involve neither prohibition nor repression, but rather a reminder and a little self-discipline. The putting aside of contrary desires that is involved is done with awareness of those desires, and is thus suppression rather than repression.

Then there are day to day moral judgements about things that just come up and need to be responded to. If a dog comes up to me barking, should I respond defensively, looking for a stick, should I try to be friendly to the dog despite its aggressive stance, or should I try to ignore it? How much priority should I give to returning that phone call when I don't really feel like it? How should I vote? Should I have another piece of chocolate cake? The fact that we may not be thinking of these as 'moral' decisions when we make them does not stop them having a moral element. They involve priorities in value, including the question of how much priority to give to my own desires when these do not feel particularly open to moral challenges. How much should I impose on myself?

Ethical practice always has to be realistic in responding to such questions. Ethical considerations might push us a little way beyond our habitual approaches – but going too far beyond them is liable to produce a reaction. There is thus always a balance to be struck in each case between challenge and realism. We also have to choose between different sorts of challenges at every turn. Do we give priority to what our society most expects? To bringing about better consequences? To following principles we have committed ourselves to?

To becoming more virtuous? In each case we need to do what stretches us most but is also compatible with a realistic capacity for moral change.

The Middle Way, then, is always applicable in every judgement in which we can bring it to awareness. We are constantly navigating between different priorities, any of which threaten to petrify into metaphysical commitment. Perhaps our prime practice, underlying all the others, is to always find that strait between the two rocks.

Summary
- Ethical practice is integrative because it involves addressing causes of conflict between desires that are engaging with different conditions
- An ethical practice involves being prepared to challenge the moral assumptions and habits of your community
- Ethical practice may involve a principle, but balance is required in applying this principle appropriately
- Ethical practice also involves a balance between challenge and realism about our capabilities for sustained change

Further Reading
My book *A New Buddhist Ethics* offers a detailed discussion of Middle Way practice in relation to a whole range of areas in which we may need to make moral decisions. Despite the title and some references to Buddhism, its basis of judgement is the Middle Way rather than Buddhist tradition.

The work of Peter Singer can be generally recommended on many aspects of practical ethics, despite its utilitarian frame, as he brings a range of conditions to our attention of a kind that people are otherwise likely to ignore. Some especially useful books of his are *Practical Ethics* and *Animal Liberation.*

Politics

My own earliest involvement in politics was as part of the Cambridge University Green Party. I listened to many idealistic words, and delivered recycled leaflets around the terraces of Cambridge, avoiding vicious dogs and trudging through the rain. After a while, though, it seemed an ineffective use of time to give it to a tiny party with (at that time) no chance of making a difference, so I let it go. Since then I have never been directly involved in party politics, though I have supported pressure groups and taught politics – and of course voted, not always for the same party.

Whatever the circumstances in which you get involved in politics, the likelihood of making a positive difference is limited. Whilst other activities often fulfil their goals incrementally (e.g. if you make a patchwork quilt, you can see progress with each new patch sewn on to it), with politics you can work away but fail to make any difference to political decision making. If you don't get your favoured candidate into office, or if your campaign fails to get enough support, you have achieved little, except perhaps at best some temporary consciousness-raising. So why do it?

The most important reasons for doing it involve principles. Even if the probability of a good consequence is small, you will be "doing your bit". The objective justification for "doing your bit" is not based on consequential reasoning, but on Kantian reasoning – that is, on the idea that you should not make an exception of yourself, but should act in the way you would prefer everyone else to act. This is not a principle that should be adopted absolutely, but this kind of reasoning can help to stretch us into greater objectivity.

If we don't want to take part in politics, but still want political decision-making to be improved, we are effectively leaving it to someone else, and exempting ourselves from political responsibility. This may be fair enough if an honest assessment of our strengths indicates that we would be better devoting our energies to other areas. In my own case, I have concluded that I am much better suited to being a political theoretician than a politician, but that I can make some indirect difference to political outcomes by seeking to stimulate other people's thinking about politics.

Even if you are better suited to political activity than I am, it is a hard road. At every junction there are compromises. Firstly, to get involved in a political party, you will have to compromise your beliefs in order to find common cause with that party. Secondly, in order to achieve political office or achieve any other political outcome (such as a change in legislation) you will have to engage in realistic negotiation in which much of what you sought to achieve may have to be bartered away as the price of achieving anything. The further away you get from your original motives, the greater the chance of alienation, as these motives can get buried by political contingencies.

Sometimes that process of negotiation can be an integrative one – a dialectic in which the best of different viewpoints are combined to produce a more objective viewpoint. There is always something to be learned from an opposing viewpoint, some way in which it addresses conditions that can be incorporated into your own. To approach political negotiation with maximum objectivity, then, your own political position needs to be provisional rather than rigidly ideological. However, if you adopt too open an approach, your opponent may just take advantage of this to try to take control of the situation. All too often, political negotiation involves not so much a discourse in which both sides are trying to reach the best solution, but a compromise between two positions of power in which each tries to get the maximum that the situation allows. Where this happens, one needs to follow a difficult Middle Way between playing the power game on the one hand and giving way to it on the other.

A politician caught up in a power game can rapidly lose the degree of integration that he or she may have started with. As the famous dictum of Lord Acton has it: "power corrupts". Power corrupts, though, not because the exercise of power is itself corrupting, but because when our dominant desires encounter less resistance from the conditions, there is no negative feedback mechanism to challenge it. The unintegrated ruling desire may thus continue to repress all other alternatives. For democratic politicians in public office, the opposition provides a check to this process by limiting and challenging power – though it does this rather crudely and often ineffectively. Whilst a politician seeks only to beat the opposition rather than learn from it, he or she is only playing a power game rather than integrative politics, even if it is a power game constrained by the mechanisms of democracy.

But that does not mean that integrative politics is impossible. In integrative politics, the use of power is subjugated to a more integrated position. This is likely to be supported by politicians using other integrative practices, and allowing them to affect their policies. Think of the difference it would make if all politicians meditated, and scrutinised all their political reasoning using advanced critical thinking skills! This, for one, would make them much more aware of the strengths of their opponents' beliefs, and less locked into metaphysical ways of thinking – whether these consist of traditional ideological thinking or just the egoism of power. Politicians who can think more flexibly might begin to address the variety of problems in the world more effectively, as well as engaging in more effective negotiations with other flexible politicians. Politicians in office may still have to use power, for example against invaders or criminals – but not against each other.

However, an integrative politics cannot arise if those who understand the value of integration keep passing the responsibility for political affairs to those who are merely ambitious. There are many examples of deluded and unscrupulous politicians, but also many who evidently had a high degree of integration that they used to great effect – Gandhi and Nelson Mandela being obvious examples. Integrative politics is possible, but incredibly hard. It requires heroes.

If you follow a political path, then, do it with integration. Whatever party you support and whatever ideologies you work with, take them as provisional tools rather than final answers. Follow the Middle Way between idealistic ineffectuality and hard-nosed political realism. Maintain a personal integrative practice to provide a perspective beyond politics.

Meanwhile, the rest of us who are not political heroes cannot entirely give up our share of responsibility for politics. As we saw in the 'levels of integration' section, political and personal integration are inextricably linked, so we cannot simply turn our back on the political. If we try to do so, our inaction will still have a political effect. If we are trying to follow the Middle Way we will not be ideologists, but we will be actively seeking solutions through an integrative process. That may involve working in parties or pressure groups, or it may involve just joining a larger political discourse and using our vote.

Summary
- A Kantian form of reasoning, in which we avoid making an exception of ourselves, provides a basic reason for thinking that we all have some responsibility for politics
- A difficult balance – the Middle Way – is involved in engaging with political power play whilst maintaining a more integrated perspective beyond the conflict it implies
- Maintaining integrative practice whilst seeking political office is so difficult that it constitutes a positively heroic path
- Our personal integration, and other types of political activity, can still have a positive effect on the wider integration of society even if we do not seek office

Further Reading
There is a discussion of integrative politics in chapter 9 of *Truth on the Edge*. There are also sections on integrative politics at the end of each of volumes 2, 3 and 4 of the *Middle Way Philosophy* series.

An understanding of political philosophy can be very helpful in thinking critically about the best approach to politics. There are many introductions to political philosophy, but I would particularly recommend Geoffrey Thomas's *Introduction to Political Philosophy.*

Life and Death

I am sometimes asked whether Middle Way Philosophy offers a meaning of life, and what it has to say about death. I have often been hesitant in trying to offer perspectives on these kinds of questions, because there is such a long tradition of unhelpful metaphysical speculation about them. However, I think the Middle Way can be applied helpfully here, if only to challenge that tradition of speculation and point us back to experience.

If we are to avoid metaphysics, there can be no meaning to life as a whole beyond the meaning that we experience. That may sound like a familiar truism – that the meaning of life is just what we make it. However, the Middle Way implies a couple of other points here as well. Not only is there no absolute metaphysical meaning to life, but there is no denial of meaning either – life is not meaningless, but rather full of the meaning we find in it. The other crucial point is that meaning is an incremental matter. We are not going to find meaning all at once, as a solution to all our struggles to find meaning. Rather, we can gradually increase the meaningfulness we encounter in life.

I suggest, also, that this incremental meaningfulness is found with our degree of integration. The meaning and value we find in life as a whole, after all, need be no different from the meaning and value we find in different specific things in life: for example, the momentary value we find in stroking a pet, or embracing someone we love. The problem with getting a meaning of life as a whole from these experiences is not that they are not meaningful in themselves, but that this meaning is momentary, and perhaps in conflict with the lack of meaning we may experience at other times. When I'm feeling frustrated in the office later on, the embrace of the early morning is already gone from my awareness.

Thus it seems that we should gradually find more meaning in life the more we become integrated, whether that integration is of desire (bringing our energies together), meaning (bringing our sense of significance together), or belief (bringing our views of the world together). The more we are integrated, the less likely we are to be caught up in inner conflict and frustration, and thus the more likely we are, on average and on the whole, to find life unified, meaningful and fulfilling.

This fulfilment is always relative to the circumstances we find ourselves in. If, for example, you are a citizen of Aleppo being constantly bombed by Syrian government forces during the Syrian civil war, you will spend most of your energy just dealing with extremely difficult and stressful external conditions. However, there will still be more or less integrated ways that you can respond to these conditions. The meaningfulness of your life in such circumstances could only really be measured against what it might have been in different circumstances, whether those circumstances were reasonably secure or even over-protected – not against some abstract absolute. Some people can be destroyed by difficulties, while others gain an intense sense of fulfilment by responding in an integrated way to them.

One of the basic conditions of difficult circumstances in life is the ever-present threat of death. Like other conditions in life, it seems that the key question is whether we can accept death and respond to it in a balanced way, rather than anything about death itself. Speculation about death itself is just a distraction from the Middle Way – whether such speculation involves beliefs about an afterlife (or reincarnation), or the denial of such beliefs. Our living experience gives us no purchase at all in justifying either affirmation or denial of afterlife beliefs, so, for example, the amount of debate about rebirth that distracts Buddhists who are otherwise interested in practising the Middle Way is rather unfortunate.

Death itself seems to be just a condition of life. It is something we are often inclined to forget that it is the temporariness of our living experience that makes it meaningful to us. An eternity of pleasure could be no more meaningful to a breathing, changing creature than an eternity of suffering, as we can only grasp the idea of pleasure or suffering in relation to an experience in which things change. The idea of such an eternity is thus just a symbolic abstraction. In practice, our pleasures are pleasurable and our pains painful only because they are impermanent, and the same could be said for life as a whole.

So, death is just a condition of life. It may be one that causes us anxiety, but anxiety is just another term for conflict between a part of us that is attached to living experience and a part that recognises the inevitability of death. If we can still that conflict, through integrative practice of one kind or another, there seems to be no reason why we should not make progress in stilling our fear of death.

I understand the sentiment that leads Dylan Thomas to write
Do not go gentle into that good-night,
But rage, rage against the dying of the light!
I read his poem as a protest against passivity and morbidity. It is possible to be too passive in the face of death, or too obsessed with the question of death. If we swap the immediate experience of living for a mere abstract idea of how we might adapt to death, we are merely distracting ourselves from the full use of the life that is available to us. However, I think Thomas's mistake is to identify the acceptance of death with one partial feeling we have in life. Instead, I think acceptance of death probably comes through integration of our different desires in life. We do not have to fight against our fear of death, but rather incorporate the energy of that fear into an overall recognition that we can live life better in a full acceptance of its conditions – and those conditions include death.

Summary

- The Middle Way implies that the meaning of life is not found in metaphysical ideas beyond our experience.

- Instead the meaning of life must be incremental and dependent on integration of the values we already feel.
- Similarly, speculation about the afterlife or its denial is not helpful in engaging with the fact of death.
- Instead, if we can integrate our responses to life, this will also imply a recognition of death as a basic condition of life.

Further Reading

I have not written elsewhere about this topic myself. I can recommend Thomas Nagel's accessible discussion in the last two chapters of *What Does it All Mean?*

5. Conclusion

Migglism (Middle Way Philosophy) is not a therapy, but it binds together therapies. It is not a scientific theory, because it is primarily directed towards developing the judgement of individuals. It is not a religion, because it does not appeal exclusively to one religious tradition or source of insight. It is not a political ideology, because it has applications at all levels of individual experience as well as in our collective life. It is not a philosophy in the narrow sense used by analytic philosophers, because it is practical and prescriptive. Nevertheless it offers a frame of reference with implications for therapy, science, religion, politics and philosophy. It is not disconnected from the existing traditions of practice in any of these areas, but rather seeks to acknowledge the degree of objectivity in all of them and offer a critical approach to understanding the nature of further progress.

Middle Way Philosophy is instead a method: a method of developing objectivity (i.e. addressing conditions better) by avoiding metaphysical assumptions of all kinds. This avoidance demands rigour, because metaphysical beliefs constantly attempt to lay claim to the middle ground and appropriate the Middle Way. I have met people who assured me that the Middle Way is really the same as Aristotle, or really the same as Thomas Aquinas, or the same as Marxism, or (of course) the same as Buddhism. An introductory book of this kind is not the place to go into details as to why all these approaches, whilst all having their insights, fall far short of the Middle Way. In the end, balance is not at their hearts. In the case of Buddhism, it took me a long time to conclude this, and it was a hard conclusion to reach – that Buddhism has departed too far from giving practical priority to the Middle Way, and introduced too many alternative metaphysical elements, to lay claim to it. A discussion of my conclusions about Buddhism when measured up against the Middle Way can be found in my book *The Trouble with Buddhism*.

So, the Middle Way is not Buddhism – it is more universal than that – but there is no reason why Buddhists cannot practise it, and indeed many aspire to do so. I welcome the fact that they seek to practice the Middle Way, but suggest that they are hindered in doing so by metaphysical commitments in Buddhism. Only if Buddhism were reformed to clearly avoid commitments to beliefs like the enlightenment of the Buddha, karma and rebirth, or the special authority of gurus, could it more closely become a vehicle for the Middle Way.

There is also no reason why people from any other traditions should not practise the Middle Way, for every tradition offers resources for addressing certain conditions, and the cultural conditioning offered by any tradition in our lives needs to be developed rather than repressed. What holds one back, whether in religious traditions like Christianity, Islam or Hinduism, or political traditions like Socialism or Conservatism, or scientific, philosophical, artistic and social traditions, is metaphysical commitment, wherever it is found. The exclusive identification of metaphysical commitment with religion is the major error of the new atheists: for we all have our metaphysical legacies to deal with, but we all also have our veins of pragmatism and openness to experience.

Middle Way Philosophy thus offers the potential to unite opposed traditions, not through shallow universalism, but on the contrary through the rigorous criticism of elements of those traditions that do not accord with experience, and are based on dogma and groupthink. Universal harmony cannot be achieved without addressing the conditions of conflict. Merely picking out the bits of metaphysics that different traditions appear to have in common (when loosely interpreted), for example, does little to address the conditions of conflict between them. Instead, thinkers within each tradition need to engage in *even-handed* critique: not just of the other chap's metaphysics (which is always more evident) but also of their own. To avoid being merely negative, such critique needs to be accompanied by shared practices that put opposed believers in touch with a shared meaning based on their embodied natures, and seeks to integrate their energies.

Middle Way Philosophy thus seems to offer our best hope for overcoming conflict and mobilising shared energy to address problems across the world. Appeals to metaphysical values, such as those of religion or national honour, will never achieve this, because whenever they appeal to metaphysics they repress other values and produce conflict. However much metaphysical ideologies talk about peace, then, it is not their ideals, but the way they conceptualise and justify them, that nevertheless produces war.

Science, if it continues to exclude value and understands its role only in terms of representational beliefs about nature, will also not succeed in addressing conflicts. Rather, if it merely describes conflicts and opposing beliefs, it will tend to entrench those conflicts by implicitly communicating the equal justification of different metaphysical positions, and offering no way to judge between them. Science's own attendant dogmas of *naturalism*, representationalism, *materialism* and determinism often also put science in conflict with religious traditions rather than producing the conditions for integration.

It is only when science, religion, or any other tradition is interpreted as a method of incrementally objective investigation through experience that it can overcome these conflicts. But that requires such traditions to avoid metaphysics – thus implicitly following the Middle Way.

I lay no personal claim on Middle Way Philosophy. Whilst it does seem to be the case that nobody else is writing explicitly about it at present, with what I would regard as all the key departure points brought together, I owe all of these departure points to others, most of whom have investigated the conditions far more closely than I have: for example to the Buddha (and many Buddhists), the sceptics, Lakoff and Johnson, Jung, pragmatist philosophy, McGilchrist and Taleb. I am just a synthesiser. Beyond this, every major thinker in every tradition has something to offer, not only in their insights but also in their errors. Looking to the future, I also think of Middle Way Philosophy as a vast potential field of investigation and practice, the development of which has hardly begun.

It is to engage others in the development and practice of the Middle Way that I have started the Middle Way Society, a group still in its infancy. If you share the overall vision of the Middle Way as the method for the achievement of objectivity of all kinds, then I invite you to join me in the study and practice of the Middle Way within the society. This step would not require you to renounce any tradition in which you are already engaged, but only its metaphysical authority. I fully expect many of the details of Middle Way Philosophy as I have developed it so far to be superseded by the more adequate work of others, who may disagree with me on the interpretation. It is the overall intuition of the primacy of the Middle Way, and a commitment to preserve that primacy against any kind of metaphysical appropriation, which I hope the society will share.

The society can work at all levels, from those who want to contribute to the development of Middle Way Philosophy intellectually to those who merely share a degree of inspiration and wish to practise the Middle Way with others. There are a very wide range of spheres in which the Middle Way can be applied. However, the first steps are to develop a community both online (see **www.middlewaysociety.org**) and on retreat, as well as over time in more localised groups. The Middle Way is not just a set of ideas, but a set of practices in which members of a community can support each other. I invite you to join that community.

Glossary

Absolute A claim without incrementality (q.v.).

Absolutism A moral theory that claims to have a source of moral certainty (e.g. God, reason etc)

Agnosticism The deliberate avoidance of either accepting or rejecting a claim, particularly a metaphysical claim. In Middle Way Philosophy this term implies *hard agnosticism*, based on a recognition of the impossibility of evidence for metaphysics. It does not imply either indecisiveness or an expectation of further evidence.

Archetype A common psychological function that tends to be associated universally with certain general types of symbol (e.g. the Shadow is the psychological function of rejecting what lies beyond current ego-identifications)

Buddhism The term 'Buddhist' as used throughout this book refers to beliefs or practices that appeal to the authority of the Buddha's enlightenment or of the Buddhist tradition

Cognitive bias A tendency towards a particular type of misjudgement found in all or most people. A large number of such biases have been identified by psychology

Cognitive model A coherent set of representations (q.v.), dependent on linked beliefs and specific metaphorical extensions (q.v.), and creating a specific and limited context for some aspects of meaning (e.g. 'Tuesday' is given meaning by a cognitive model of time including a seven-day week)

Conditions The way things appear to be as they impact on us from the outside (or inside) world beyond experience. Many writers use the terms 'reality' and 'nature' for this concept, both of which I prefer to avoid because of their metaphysical connotations.

Confirmation bias The cognitive bias (q.v.) of limiting the evidence we consider to that which will fit our prior assumptions

Desire Motive, drive or energy that might actually or potentially lead us to action, whether conscious or unconscious.

Determinism The belief that all events are inevitable, including our choices, so that we have no freewill

Dogma, Dogmatism The psychological expression of metaphysics, where beliefs are held strongly because they are thought to be intrinsically true, regardless of experience. A dogma is a belief held in this way.

Ego Our experience of having wishes and identifications (with both ourselves and others), including our desire to continue existing as a self

Embodied meaning An understanding of meaning based on a recognition of how the physical body creates meaningfulness.

Epistemology The study of our beliefs and their justification

Experiential adequacy The extent to which our experience is able to understand conditions without interference from dogmatic assumptions

Falsification The justifiable (but not certain) conclusion that a theory is wrong because of its incompatibility with evidence. In Middle Way Philosophy falsification can be undertaken by individuals, not just by scientists using strict research methods.

Fragmentation of meaning The separation of meanings (i.e. symbol-attachments) so that one fails to recognise the other, whether within the individual or between individuals

Group An association involving shared identifications between two or more people.

Identification The sense of possessiveness towards oneself, a person or an object, making them in some sense "me" or "mine".

Incrementality The conceptualisation of qualities as a matter of degree on a spectrum, rather than as absolutes that are either existent or non-existent.

Integration The uniting of conflicting desires through the reforming of the beliefs with which they are associated into greater objectivity

Justification The finding of adequate (though not certain) reasons to believe or disbelieve a claim. In Middle Way Philosophy this requires both coherence and awareness of fallibility.

Materialism The belief that everything we experience is made of ultimately physical stuff obeying the laws of physics

Meaning The habitual attachment of desire to a symbol through the neural networks, physical associations, and cognitive models we have developed.

Metaphorical extension Pattern of association between a new symbol and a more basic *schema* (q.v.) that makes the new symbol meaningful in embodied experience

Metaphysics Positive or negative claims that are asserted without any possible justification from experience, using absolute claims or absolute sources of justification (or their denial).

Middle Way A philosophical and practical approach that avoids both positive and negative metaphysical claims, seeking to address conditions by adopting beliefs that go beyond the assumptions of both sides.

Middle Way Philosophy A fuller development of the implications of the Middle Way, which also makes use of concepts such as integration and embodied meaning.

Migglism A shortened synonym for Middle Way Philosophy

Moral objectivity The aspect of objectivity (q.v.) that is applied to moral judgements as to how to live and act (not a distinct type of objectivity, but a way that objectivity in general can be applied).

Naturalism The belief that science can represent reality by discovering laws of nature, justified by 'objective' factual evidence that rules out values. This is metaphysical both because the idea that we can attain absolute 'laws of nature' neglects the insights of scepticism (q.v.) and because it falsely separates facts from values.

Negative metaphysics Claims about the non-existence of a metaphysical (q.v.) entity beyond experience.

Objectivity The incremental (q.v.) quality of judgement that enables us to understand and address conditions (q.v.). In Middle Way Philosophy this term does **not** mean 'a God's eye view of the universe'.

Positive Metaphysics Claims in support of the existence of a metaphysical (q.v.) entity beyond experience.

Pragmatism A philosophical approach that emphasises practical usefulness rather than adherence to an absolute view of how things are. In Middle Way Philosophy this practical usefulness is understood in a long-term sense.

Projection The process by which an object is assumed to have the meaning of an archetype, despite the fact that the psychological function is in the viewer, not the object

Provisionality The psychological state of holding beliefs flexibly enough to enable them to be changed in the light of new evidence. This also requires the avoidance of metaphysical beliefs, because they cannot be held in this way.

Relativism The denial of moral or other types of truth. Moral relativism implies that only personal choice or social conventions are sources of value, and that there is no justification for preferring one to another.

Representation A mental image which is believed to be equivalent to a state of affairs of some kind beyond the mind

Representationalism The belief that language has only cognitive meaning gained from its representative relationship with the world (for example through truth-conditions).

Repression The denial of one desire by another, in which the dominant desire attempts unsuccessfully to completely eliminate the subordinate one.

Scepticism The belief that no claims (or their denials) can be certain.

Schema Basic pattern in embodied experience that can be associated with symbols to make them meaningful. E.g. the 'source-path-goal' schema makes the word 'path' meaningful.

Scientific Objectivity The aspect of objectivity (q.v.) which is applied to theoretical judgements about the universe using scientific method (not a distinct type of objectivity, but a way that objectivity in general may be applied). Some of this objectivity may be individual, some the quality of scientists as a group.

Secular Non-religious or anti-religious. *Secularism* normally involves anti-religious tendencies.

Solipsism The belief that one is alone in the universe and no other minds exist

Suppression The aware and temporary adoption of one desire as dominant over another, and denial of immediate expression to the subordinate desire. This is distinguished from repression (q.v.) by continuing recognition of the subordinate desire.

Symbol Any object that is experienced as meaningful, e.g. words, pictures, sounds, other significant objects

Truth on the edge The regulative idea of an ultimate state of affairs, which is meaningful but cannot be the object of justified assertions.

Bibliography

This bibliography lists fuller details of all the books mentioned in the 'further reading' sections.

My own books

(These can all be purchased from **http://www.lulu.com/spotlight/robertupeksa**)

Ellis, Robert M (2011) *A Theory of Moral Objectivity*: Lulu, Raleigh (originally a Ph.D. thesis accredited in 2001)

Ellis, Robert M (2011) *North Cape: Selected Poems of a Poet Turned Philosopher:* Lulu, Raleigh

Ellis, Robert M (2011) *The Trouble with Buddhism:* Lulu, Raleigh

Ellis, Robert M (2011) *A New Buddhist Ethics:* Lulu, Raleigh

Ellis, Robert M (2011) *Truth on the Edge: A Brief Western Philosophy of the Middle Way:* Lulu, Raleigh

Ellis, Robert M (2012) *Middle Way Philosophy 1: The Path of Objectivity:* Lulu, Raleigh

Ellis, Robert M (2013) *Middle Way Philosophy 2: The Integration of Desire:* Lulu, Raleigh

Ellis, Robert M (2013) *Middle Way Philosophy 3: The Integration of Meaning:* Lulu, Raleigh

Buddhist Scriptures

Anguttara Nikaya: *Numerical Discourses of the Buddha,* trans. Nyanaponika Thera & Bodhi: Buddhist Publications Society, Kandy/ Altamira Press, Walnut Creek

Majjhima Nikaya: *The Middle Length Discourses of the Buddha,* trans. Ñanamoli and Bodhi: Wisdom Books, Boston

Other books

Bondurant, Joan (1958) *Conquest of Violence*: Princeton University Press, Princeton

Moore, Brooke Noel and Parker, Richard (2011) *Critical Thinking*: McGraw Hill, New York

House, Adrian (2000) *Francis of Assisi:* Chatto & Windus, London

Inwood, Brad and Gerson, L.P (1997) *Hellenistic Philosophy: Introductory Readings:* Hackett, Indianapolis

Johnson, Mark (2007) *The Meaning of the Body*: University of Chicago Press, Chicago

Jung, Carl (1959) *Aion:* Routledge, London

Jung, Carl (1959) *The Archetypes and the Collective Unconscious*: Routledge, London

Jung, Carl (1960) *On the Nature of the Psyche:* Routledge, London

Jung, Carl (1983) *Memories, Dreams, Reflections:* Flamingo, London

Kamalashila (1992) *Meditation: the Buddhist Way of Tranquillity and Insight*: Windhorse Publications, Glasgow

Kuhn, Thomas (1996) *The Structure of Scientific Revolutions*: University of Chicago Press, Chicago

Kuzminski, Adrian (2010) *Pyrrhonism: How the Ancient Greeks Reinvented Buddhism*: Lexington Books, Lanham

Lakatos, Imre (1974) 'Falsification and the Methodology of Scientific Research Programmes' from *Criticism and the Growth of Knowledge* ed. I Lakatos and A. Musgrave, Cambridge University Press, Cambridge

McGilchrist, Iain (2009) *The Master and his Emissary*: Yale University Press, New Haven & London

Midgley, Mary (1991) *Can't we make Moral Judgements?* Bristol Classical Press, Bristol

Nagel, Thomas (1986) *The View from Nowhere*: Oxford University Press, New York

Nagel, Thomas (1987) *What Does it All Mean?* Oxford University Press, Oxford

Ñanamoli, Bhikkhu (1992) *The Life of the Buddha*: Buddhist Publications Society, Kandy

Singer, Peter (1993) *Practical Ethics:* Cambridge University Press, Cambridge

Singer, Peter (1995) *Animal Liberation:* Pimlico, London

Taleb, Nassim Nicholas (2012) *Antifragile:* Penguin, London

Thomas, Geoffrey (2000) *Introduction to Political Philosophy*: Duckworth, London

Thomson, Anne (2008) *Critical Reasoning: A Practical Introduction:* Routledge, London